C A P S T O N E

Stay Smart!

CAPSTONE

Smart

THINGS TO KNOW ABOUT...

Six Sigma

ANDREW BERGER

The right of Andrew Berger to be identified as the author of this book has been
asserted in accordance with the Copyright, Designs and Patents Act 1988

First published 2003   by
Capstone Publishing Limited (a Wiley Company)
The Atrium
Southern Gate
Chichester
West Sussex
PO19 8SQ
www.wileyeurope.com

Reprinted March 2004

CIP catalogue records for this book are available from the British Library and the
US Library of Congress

ISBN 1-84112-433-8

Typeset by Forewords, 109 Oxford Road, Cowley, Oxford
Printed and bound in Great Britain by CPI Antony Rowe, Eastbourne
This book is printed on acid-free paper responsibly manufactured from sustainable forestry
in which at least two trees are planted for each one used for paper production.

Contents

What is Smart?

The *Smart* series is a new way of learning. *Smart* books will improve your understanding and performance in some of the critical areas you face to-day like *customers, strategy, change, e-commerce, brands, influencing skills, knowledge management, finance, teamworking, partnerships.*

Smart books summarize accumulated wisdom as well as providing original cutting-edge ideas and tools that will take you out of theory and into action.

The widely respected business guru Chris Argyris points out that even the most intelligent individuals can become ineffective in organizations. Why? Because we are so busy working that we fail to learn about ourselves. We stop reflecting on the changes around us. We get sucked into the patterns of behavior that have produced success for us in the past, not realizing that it may no longer be appropriate for us in the fast-approaching future.

There are three ways the Smart series helps prevent this happening to you:

- by increasing your self-awareness

- by developing your understanding, attitude and behavior

- by giving you the tools to challenge the status quo that exists in your organization.

Smart people need smart organizations. You could spend a third of your career hopping around in search of the Holy Grail, or you could begin to create your own smart organization around you today.

Finally a reminder that books don't change the world, people do. And although the *Smart* series offers you the brightest wisdom from the best practitioners and thinkers, these books throw the responsibility on you to *apply* what you're learning in your work.

Because the truly smart person knows that reading a book is the start of the process and not the end . . .

As Eric Hoffer says, "In times of change, learners inherit the world, while the learned remain beautifully equipped to deal with a world that no longer exists."

David Firth
Smartmaster

Acknowledgements

This book has been the work of many people and it is right that their contributions should be clearly recognized. I would like to thank Andy Bruce, Susan Currie and Mark Edwards for their support in embarking on the project. Without their hard work we would never have started. Ken Langdon and Neil Wilson provided much of the work needed to get the book into the right shape and structure. Linda Nuthall provided the intellectual horsepower required to integrate the case study and project tools into a coherent story. This is the second book we have worked on together and it was (again) a pleasure. Many thanks to Linda, Andy and Susan for their ongoing contributions to the editing. Thanks also to Catriona Williams of Skillset for the excellent advice on building a Six Sigma business and for constantly keeping my feet firmly on the ground. A final thank you also to Mark Allin and John Moseley at Capstone Wiley for giving us the opportunity to write the book as part of their Smart series.

Preface

John Kelly put the phone down after a very uncomfortable conversation with the Chairman of one of his main customers. The message had been stark. Working from a briefing from their IT department, the Chairman had run through a catalogue of missed delivery dates of equipment sold by Blue Computers, the company of which John was the managing director.

> "We have had frequent problems with your failed promises. When your equipment has not arrived on time, we have to put our improvement plans on hold because your people failed again. Last weekend, we had a large mobile crane sitting around waiting to lift some of your equipment into one of our city offices. It never arrived. This is costing us a lot of money, John, and if you cannot improve things, then, despite the long relationship between our two companies, we are going to look elsewhere."

And that was just the repeatable part before she got upset.

The situation had been getting steadily worse, John knew, with poor predictability of delivery dates and times a constant headache; along with almost daily crises where a customer had taken delivery of hardware and software only to find that it did not meet the specification that the salespeople had promised. Even without the customer satisfaction issue, the problem was also having a huge impact on cashflow – late delivery obviously threw the cash forecast out. Beside which, customers are not going to be particularly co-operative in meeting their payment obligations when they are feeling badly let down.

Still, John had taken some action. David Spencer was the latest young high flyer. He had been seconded to John's office from the London sales team where he had cut a swathe through the East End, clocking up more new business clients from cold calling than anyone before. From there he had moved into managing a key international account, and had achieved a mighty increase in sales along with producing a series of innovative solutions for the customer. John had added David to his staff team with a remit to sort these delivery problems out. John had explained the project simply – "Make it the rule that deliveries occur on time with a minimal failure rate, and no excuses. Oh, and make sure that any expenditure involved in doing it has a clear return on investment, we cannot continue just chucking money at this."

He had sent a note to David via his secretary Penny adding that he wanted him to get much better co-operation between the sales force and the operations side of the business. "There is a natural suspicion between sales and production," Penny had demurred "I doubt he'll be able to change that." "He'll be back on the street if he doesn't," muttered John darkly as he returned to his office, "After all he got me to send him on that Six Sigma course," he added, "And that's supposed to be the latest cure for situations like this. This looks like a great opportunity to see if this Black Belt stuff works."

Throughout this book you will see how Dave Spencer uses Six Sigma tools and techniques to address the problems that face Blue Computers. He will take you through how he and his team solve problems, develop solutions and document their progress. You will see how he and John Kelly, his project sponsor, manage their way through the approvals and reviews that are key drivers of Six Sigma success.

You will also see how Dave Spencer uses his new-found expertise in Six Sigma project delivery to develop new skills and career opportunities. As a Six Sigma Black Belt, Dave's knowledge increases his value to Blue Computers. This opens up new opportunities for working in other areas of the company, promotion and increased pay and bonuses. Dave also starts to open up a valuable network with other Six Sigma Black Belts in other companies that are undertaking similar Six Sigma projects.

Introduction

Continuous improvement projects using Six Sigma have been gathering momentum for some years now, with some companies, the pioneering ones, attempting to implement it on a corporate-wide basis. Other, less pioneering companies, are using it to solve major problem areas within the organization, and some are just trying it out with a limited number of people involved on a particular problem – the softly, softly approach.

Six Sigma is certainly being credited with some very impressive financial benefits by companies that have been in the forefront of its implementation. GE and Honeywell, for example, claim to have delivered financial benefits of more than $1 billion through Six Sigma, with other companies such as ABB, Texas Instruments and Polaroid pitching in with benefits in the $100–800 million range according to the American Society for Quality (ASQ). We are seeing Six Sigma initiatives in a wide range of companies such as 3M, Ford, Home Depot, Dow Chemicals and J.P. Morgan Chase. Six Sigma is growing across different industries and geographies as more management teams address their companies' need for continuous improvement.

Where does Six Sigma get its name?

The name derives from the statistical term that uses the lower case Greek letter σ (sigma) to mean standard deviation. If you improve the sigma or standard deviation of any process you are in effect reducing the failure or defect rate of that process. For instance, if you are in the business of selling mobile telephones, and you receive a return rate of 23%, because of deliveries of the wrong product or products with defects, you are being successful 77% of the time. The sigma calculator or table (see the table at the end of this book) gives you a sigma value of 2.25. By looking hard at what the customer expects from the delivery of the product and modifying your production and distribution processes, you could improve your success rate to say 96% or 3.25 sigma. But would that be good enough?

Six Sigma sets out to deliver a quality level of 3.4 defects per million opportunities (DPMO). This is similar to the old five 9s description of quality – 99.999% accuracy.

Don't be put off by this statistical description; Six Sigma techniques are not new inventions, they are a collection of many existing analysis techniques that you will have seen before. This makes Six Sigma an excellent method for setting continuous improvement targets and for monitoring progress in improving any process. Six Sigma can be used for major and minor improvement projects. You can use it to set efficiency targets for a

How do I explain Sigma levels and variability?

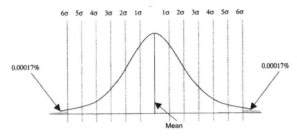

Process Sigma can be applied to any process where the number of 'defects' or 'failures to meet specifications' can be counted. It can also be applied to multi-step processes where the aim is to measure overall process performance.

- *Process Sigma*: This is an expression of yield that is based on the number of defects per one million defect opportunities (DPMO).
- *Unit*: The item produced or the process outcome.
- *Defect*: Any unit that does not meet specification.
- *Defect opportunity*: A measurable chance for a defect to occur.

Put simply, the basic aim in Six Sigma is to improve average performance and to tighten up variability of performance.

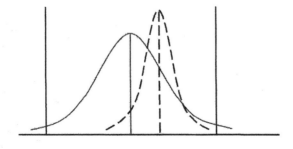

> Six Sigma has changed the DNA of GE – it is now the way we work – in everything we do and in every product we design.
>
> GE, The Roadmap to Customer Impact

whole range of business activities from manufacturing to back offices in banks and other financial institutions. Government departments and hospitals could also benefit from applying Six Sigma techniques to their high volume processes.

What is Six Sigma?

Six Sigma is a collection of fact-based tools and techniques aimed at helping a business to deliver financial benefits from continuous improvement. It consists of a set of data-driven tools and methodologies designed to significantly improve the quality of products and services delivered to customers. It is highly customer driven in that you cannot use the tools without taking the needs and wants of the customer into account. It is also facts and data driven to bring an analytical and objective, or honest, focus to improving processes.

It can be used to improve any process. Companies have delivered Six Sigma benefits from improvements in many business areas including:

- Customer satisfaction

- Product cycle times

- Manufacturing

- Distribution and delivery

- Defects reduction

What is Six Sigma? Why is it different to normal statistics?

Six Sigma represents 3.4 defects per million opportunities (DPMO). Five Sigma is 230 DPMO and Four Sigma is 6,200 DPMO. It is based on adapting a normal distribution where sigma is the standard deviation from the mean. Six Sigma tables shift normal distribution values of sigma to create an index of sigma levels where Six Sigma is 3.4 defects per million opportunities. If you want to understand the difference between a normal distribution and a Six Sigma calculation chart, just think of it being a 1.5 sigma shift to every value in the normal distribution.

Management can use Six Sigma in two main and related ways. Firstly, as a quality target for the company's processes – Six Sigma sets out a target performance level of less than 3.4 DPMO. In fact the right level of sigma will depend on the process and the economics of achieving higher levels of quality. Secondly, as an aspiration towards a culture and management system like GE's where Six Sigma is seen as a mechanism for building a culture of excellence as well as the delivery of financial benefits. This second aspiration involves setting up teams to solve specific problems on a project-by-project basis, and training a very wide group of people so that the whole organization is searching for ways of listening and reacting to the customer, seeking facts to measure current success and focusing on the issues that really affect customer satisfaction. In some organizations such as GE, Six Sigma training is a requirement for anyone hoping for a bonus or promotion. In many Six Sigma companies up to 1% of all people are trained to the Black Belt standard of accreditation.

How does a Six Sigma programme start?

Most companies going into Six Sigma start by getting senior and middle managers to attend training courses with external organizations to gain accreditation for their people. This allows them to pick up the main management roles in the teams that are appointed to achieve Six Sigma measures in target areas. Black Belts (fully trained, full-time Six Sigma advisers) are in charge of the teams. Their job is to provide the leadership in driving the Six Sigma processes through, and the expertise to facilitate good quality in the management and documentation of Six Sigma. A Green Belt may have less training than a Black Belt, and by definition is not full time on the Six Sigma process they are involved in. Green Belts continue with their normal jobs, but accept responsibility for their part in achieving Six Sigma objectives. Typically a Green Belt will accept commitment to a Six Sigma project for 10–50% of their time. They are usually team leaders and not project managers. Some companies do use Green Belts to manage projects.

Some factors are critical to the success of a Six Sigma programme and you can see them at three levels. At the highest level there is the need for senior management commitment to starting, supporting and finishing projects. This may also require them to take difficult decisions about priorities and resources. It goes without saying that all projects must be clearly linked to the achievement of agreed business imperatives. Busi-

---

SMART QUOTES

GE had another huge advantage that accelerated our quality effort. We had a company that was open to change, hungry to learn and anxious to move quickly on a good idea.

GE Annual Report 1997

ness imperatives are the overall targets that must be met if an organization is to achieve its overall mission or vision. At a project manager level, success factors are about finding the right definition of the right projects and securing the right resources to deliver the project on time and budget. At a team member level the critical success factors are training, commitment, good allocation of tasks and sharing of critical knowledge and best practices.

DMAIC – the main Six Sigma process

The project process that teams use for continuous improvement in Six Sigma is called DMAIC, pronounced 'DeMAYic'. DMAIC stands for Define – Measure & Analyse – Improve – Control. (We will talk about more advanced techniques for process innovation in Chapter 7, Design for Six Sigma). The DMAIC approach is designed to deal with processes that are generally well understood in companies but have not been rigorously analysed using numerical data, particularly financial data, to identify potential additional productivity improvements. Our rule of thumb is that companies should achieve at least a 90% success rate on continuous improvement projects. DMAIC is the best methodology for ensuring that this target is met. We will go step by step through the DMAIC process in this book. Each element in the process is designed to provide fact-based insights and clues as to what needs to be changed and how it should be done. It is worth saying at this early stage that the DMAIC process also requires an open and honest approach to change. For example, a Six Sigma culture insists on removing people's fear of blame in order to encourage them to be very open about their performance and skills and knowledge problems. The culture demands that project managers in particular signal quickly, for example, when there is a problem rather than sitting on it in the hope of finding a solution before it impacts the critical path of the project and comes to senior management attention.

Avoid the blame culture. A Greek soldier was guarding three Mig fighters, visitors from Russia, on an airstrip outside Athens. From the front of a Mig there protrudes a radio antenna. The bored guard decided to do some pull-ups on one of the antenna that happened to stand at exactly the right height for this exercise. As he jumped up he bent the antenna.

The soldier knew he had a problem but unfortunately went straight from there to an immediate solution. There were three aircraft, one with a bent antenna and two with straight antennae. The guard's solution was to quietly bend the other two into the same shape.

How do we know all this? Bad luck for him but the entire episode was recorded on security cameras. It is often better to highlight mistakes early so that they can be solved before there is greater damage.

The DMAIC process contains a series of standard activities and expected outputs. This is much more than just filling out forms, templates and charts. We will take you through the major outputs from DMAIC using templates that have been developed for Six Sigma software. These templates are built from an electronic knowledge base of best practices in Six Sigma. They encourage a culture of knowledge sharing, co-operation and project honesty. Wide access to these templates by the project sponsors and other managers involved can help to make project teams much more effective and to train people efficiently.

As you go through this book you will be encouraged to think about a business problem or a business process in your organization that needs attention. In that way you should get the most benefit of coming to an understanding of Six Sigma and the culture of continuous improvement.

What is the probability of success for our current improvement projects? Is it acceptable?

KILLER
QUESTIONS

Use an assessment based on the five key project factors that determine whether projects will be successful or not. These factors can be expressed as a simple equation:

Right financial results = right projects × right people × right process × right management decision × right knowledge sharing

If a company gets each of these key project factors right 70% of the time, the overall probability of success is only 17% ($0.7^5 = 17\%$)

If a company could improve its performance and get each of these key project factors right 95% of the time, the overall probability of success increases to 77% ($0.95^5 = 77\%$). This is an improvement of 60% in financial benefits for a 25% improvement on each factor.

What needs to change is the consistency with which companies select the right projects, resource them with the right people, manage them with the right processes, make the right management decisions and share knowledge and best practices. It is important to recognize that managing a portfolio of improvement projects requires the same attention to detail and process discipline that is demanded in other business areas such as due diligence, audit and financial management. It is about increasing the average level of performance on improvement projects and closing the gap between best and worst performances.

You need to be careful that you only apply Six Sigma levels where it makes good business sense. For instance, no one would want to fly in an aeroplane that had quality levels below Six Sigma – you wouldn't last very long! However, for some processes, four or five sigma can be totally acceptable, particularly in a situation where a small improvement in performance costs a disproportionate amount of money and effort. For instance, 230 errors per million in some processes may make more business sense than taking on more people or working extra hours. The key is being sensible about the level of sigma and recognizing that the same analytical tools can be used across a range of projects with different target sigma levels. However, try not to use this as an excuse to avoid implementing Six Sigma where it can impact critical to quality (CTQ) processes profitably.

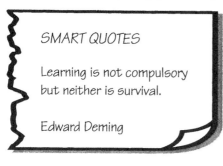

SMART QUOTES

Learning is not compulsory but neither is survival.

Edward Deming

As a first step in his project Dave Spencer had decided to look at a "voice of the customer" (VOC) analysis. He remembered what he had been taught at his Six Sigma Black Belt training: "Everything must start with the customer!" Dave knew that he must drive the project from the customer. He decided that looking at customer problems and requirements would act as a good "ice breaker" for getting the project team working together.

Starting out – listening to the voice of the customer

Six Sigma is full of jargon such as VOC and CTQ. Don't be afraid of this – most of it is actually very simple and we have a good glossary of terms at the end of the book to explain what it all means. We will try to demystify the jargon but remember there is nothing difficult about understanding Six Sigma.

CTQ involves identifying and converting customer requirements into well-defined and measurable CTQ measures. This may, for example, involve your using VOC analysis where you simply look for the words that a customer would use to describe their lack of customer satisfaction and turning them into the implications for your business and the actual customer requirement.

Throughout the book you will see Dave Spencer, the Black Belt involved in the Blue Computer case study, building up his project facts and analysis. Where required he will refer to additional material in the Six Sigma training manual. In the glossary at the end of this book there are explanations of the main terms that Six Sigma uses to define its principles and processes. There are examples of a number of the statistical techniques Six Sigma managers use throughout the book, and a number are described in the appendix. Lets start with the Voice of the Customer.

This VOC analysis comes from the first team meeting that Dave Spencer had with his project team. It is a first attempt, in the early stages of the Define phase, to expose problems that customers are having with Blue Computers.

CTQ must have clear process metrics and agreed limits to be effective.

Have we listened to the "voice of the customer?"

What is the customer saying that relates to this problem? This could be derived from complaints, responses to surveys, or other sources of direct feedback from customers

- Business implications: Try, wherever possible, to quantify the impact, although you will *do more of this further on in the process.*

- Critical customer requirement (CCR): What is the customer requirement in terms of what the supplying business actually needs to deliver?

- Critical to quality (CTQ) measures: How are we going to measure a baseline position and our improvements?

KILLER QUESTIONS

Voice of the customer	Business implications	Critical customer requirement (CCR)	Critical to quality (CTQ) measures	
1	Product arrives too early or late, needs to be "on-time"	Customer disruption, costs for "extraordinary assistance"	Delivery 100% in line with commitment	% Delivery on time in full (OTIF) accuracy
2	If product late, then payment late	Cash to cash cycle time too long	Deliver on time and use simple business rules for payment	Days outstanding accounts receivables
3	Competitors can deliver just in time (JIT)	Lose future sales. If we lost the customer who has complained most, it would cost £3 m in revenue	Supplier who can meet promises	% customer promises met % competitor OTIF performance

CTQ forms the basis of the rationale for undertaking a Six Sigma improvement project.

So, how brave are you feeling about Six Sigma? Perhaps you are a chief executive looking for a method of transforming your organization, or a senior manager like John Kelly of Blue Computers looking for a solution to a significant business problem that has affected the company for many years, or a project manager looking for a way to improve your chances of success in your next project. This book gives you in text and reference form the smart things you need to know about Six Sigma.

At the coffee break of his first team meeting, Dave Spencer felt confident that his project was going to go well. He had found himself a great team of

KILLER
QUESTIONS

Does your approach to Six Sigma combine statistics and fact-based analysis with:

- Project management skills?
- Team management skills?
- Management commitment?
- Risk management?
- A culture of continuous improvement and innovation?

If your approach is just about statistics you will fail at Six Sigma! In this book, we will show you how to get a good the balance between each of these factors.

people to work with. There was a lot to do in a short period of time but this was a team that was going to be open and honest. He was sure that he would be able to delegate a lot of work to the other team members especially the ones with Green Belt training. First, he needed to get the team thinking about opportunities for projects that would deliver hard financial benefits fast.

Dave had also been reading up about how other companies were implementing Six Sigma programmes. He had found out that GE had tied all bonuses and promotions to people who had succeeded at Black Belt training and projects. He knew it would not be long before Blue Computers would be implementing similar Human Resources processes. "If

This is not the end. It is not even the beginning of the end. But it is, perhaps, the end of the beginning.

Winston Churchill

SMART QUOTES

that's the way that people will be rewarded in future, then it makes sense to get trained and active on Six Sigma projects" he had told a colleague. "There is a new culture growing in Blue Computers and it is all about getting the right things done well. I'm going to make sure that I am going to take full advantage of this Six Sigma opportunity."

Dave's wife had noticed several job adverts in the newspaper for Six Sigma Black Belts. Given the salaries they were offering, Dave knew that there were going to be plenty of opportunities for him in future. What he needed to do was to prove himself as a successful Black Belt on this project.

1

Assessing the Potential Benefits of Six Sigma

Even medium-sized organizations can have a large portfolio of projects going on at any one time. Many of these fail to deliver on time and within budget, and even those that pass these tests rarely produce substantiated financial benefits. Six Sigma, the DMAIC process and an integrated approach can change this quickly.

The problems you could solve with Six Sigma

If you belong to an average company, there will be a lot of improvement projects currently being undertaken. You and your colleagues will be putting a lot of effort into starting projects and trying to bring them to a satisfactory conclusion. Your company will be investing a great deal of money and time in these projects. The sad fact is that 70–80% of your projects will fail to deliver their planned benefits. What is frightening is that this figure hasn't changed much over the last 10–15 years. If you would like to do something about this read on!

Six Sigma self-assessment – projects and benefits

The first thing to do is to gather some information on how well your company is performing. The potential value of Six Sigma to your organization could be very significant but we need some facts first. It may be difficult, at this stage, to understand which areas of your portfolio of improvement projects are in most need of change. We have two smart and simple self-assessment diagnostics tools designed to help you to assess your organization's potential for project process improvements and increased financial benefits. Use them with your colleagues and senior managers; you will be surprised at two things:

• How consistently people will give the same results; and

• The potential size of the improvement opportunity available to your company.

The project self-assessment diagnostic is designed to give two measures – your average performance on key project activities and the spread between best and worst performance. The second self-assessment diagnostic looks at your organization's potential for improved delivery of financial benefits.

How do you justify the effort and expenditure of a Six Sigma project?

All projects must have a justification. Most projects will be justified on the basis of financial benefits being much greater than project costs. A few projects may be justified for non-financial reasons – mainly strategic or new capability projects. All projects must be clearly linked to agreed business imperatives. It is also important that the overall portfolio of projects has strong financial benefits that can be delivered within this financial year as well as future years. The credibility of improvement projects is often determined by their ability to deliver short-term financial benefits whilst paying for and building future capabilities.

SMART ANSWERS TO TOUGH QUESTIONS

Project effectiveness self-assessment

The first diagnostic looks at how good your company is at shaping and delivering improvement projects. Assess your company's average, best and worst performance on 10 project-related questions. Use the following performance rating scale:

Performance rating for your organization

1 = Poor

2 = Average for industry/organization size

3 = Good

4 = Very Good

5 = World Class

	Average performance	Best performance	Worst performance
1. Are you good at selecting the right projects based on clear business imperatives?			
2. Are you good at generating project ideas internally and from external sources such as customers, suppliers and competitors?			
3. Are you good at appointing project managers with the right mix of project, technical and people skills?			
4. Are you effective in building good project teams and involving the right types of skills at the right time?			
5. Are you good at sharing best practices and lessons learned to improve the performance of projects?			
6. Are you good at managing operational and project workloads and resources to avoid overloading key individuals?			
7. Does senior management have clear visibility and predictability about the delivery of financial benefits of projects in this financial year?			
8. Are external advisers managed effectively? Do they really transfer knowledge to your people?			
9. Are your project teams good at managing project risks?			
10. Are you good at developing a pool of project managers for the future?			

Total score

Average spread between best and worst = (total best − total worst)/10

Mark your company's score for the average and range between best and worst on the table below. This will give you a reasonable idea of where benefits could come from in using Six Sigma tools and procedures.

Projects scorecard

Your company average score	Average score	Opportunity	Your company's average range between best and worst	Average score spread	Opportunity
	0–19	*Poor performance –* lost opportunities and low delivery of financial benefits		3–4	Improve communication and fragmentation
	20–29	*Average to good –* scope for significant increases in financial benefits		2–3	Scope for significant improvements in sharing best practices
	30–39	*Good* – scope for some improvements in financial benefits		1–2	Good sharing of best practices if average performance score is also high
	40–50	*Very good* – write a book about your company's way		0–1	Very good sharing of best practices

Financial benefits – improvement potential

The second diagnostic looks at the potential to improve the delivery of financial benefits. Assess the percentage of projects for which your organization achieves consistently good performance on five key project factors:

	Financial benefits improvement potential	How often does your company get this key project factor right? (e.g. 0.7 = 70%)
A	Right ideas and projects	
B	Right project managers and teams	
C	Right project definition and execution	
D	Right management approvals and decision making	
E	Right sharing of knowledge and best practices	
F	Your company's probability of success	Calculate $A \times B \times C \times D \times E$
G	Potential improvement in financial benefits (by achieving 95% consistently)	Calculate 77% – F

If the potential improvement is greater than 10%, the Six Sigma set of tools could make a big difference to your company's future. Academic and business research suggests that only 20–30% of improvement projects deliver planned financial benefits. Remember that this statistic has not changed over the last 10–15 years!

It is also important to be clear about the types of benefits that projects are setting out to deliver. The most desirable benefits are hard financial savings that will be delivered within this financial year. Most companies will look for at least a 1–2 year payback on projects – some want a clear payback in less than 1 year. Less certain financial benefits such as cost avoidance or project-related savings in other departments do count but they are often difficult to measure and prove. Intangible benefits such as customer and employee satisfaction can be used but they will have their enemies within the finance department. The key is to balance a portfolio of projects in a company that can deliver this year's financial targets whilst preparing the company for future successes.

Selecting the right projects

> The genius of Six Sigma is its recognition that a great many serious business problems have a at their roots mundane issues. These problems can be characterized as "hard to find and easy to fix".
>
> Dr Michael Hammer and Jeff Goding, Putting Six Sigma in Perspective, Quality Online, October 2001

SMART
PEOPLE
TO HAVE
ON YOUR
SIDE

Remember the principles of "simplicity and focus": you will need them throughout your Six Sigma projects. Put simply, it is always easier to look good and perform well when you are working on a project that has the potential to deliver value. There is nothing worse than having to expend your effort on a project that will never work! We recently asked Black Belts from over 25 companies how often their firm selected the right projects to work on. The result was frightening: only 40–50%. They were telling us that before project teams had even got working there was a good chance that they would fail.

A simple way to assess the potential for projects is impact vs. effort. The project manager and team assess the potential of the project on the basis

Impact/effort prioritization

Impact area	Summary	Score	Weighting	Weighted score
Revenue growth		3	0.4	1.2
Cost reduction/cost avoidance		3	0.4	1.2
Customer satisfaction		5	0.1	0.5
Complexity reduction		5	0.1	0.5
Total			1.0	3.4

Effort area	Summary	Score	Weighting	Weighted score
People (man day) effort		3	0.3	0.9
Direct (non-people related) costs		3	0.2	0.6
Reusability across the business		1	0.3	0.3
Requirement for external resources		3	0.2	0.6
Total			1.0	2.4
Impact/Effort Ratio				1.4

Risk adjustment	Evidence for risk and probability of success assessment	Probability of success
Probability of success for the project	We should achieve 90% on continuous improvement projects	90%
Total		90%
Risks adjusted impact/effort ratio		1.3

of its potential impact and required level of effort. Impact is mainly in financial and customer terms. Effort is defined mainly in terms of costs and people required. The scores are then weighted according to company wide weightings. The weighted scores are then adjusted for risk levels. This impact/effort calculation allows projects to be compared and prioritized against clear assessment criteria.

Multiple project opportunities can be assessed using this type of approach and mapped in a simple opportunities matrix. The aim is to prioritize those projects that have the highest impact for the least effort. As a company gets better at selecting the right projects, it can refine the selection criteria on the basis of which projects delivered the highest benefits compared to predicted scores on the impact/effort matrix.

An integrated approach to DMAIC

Dave Spencer reached for his laptop computer. He wanted to remind himself about the DMAIC methodology and was pleased that he had it all set out on an electronic knowledge base. Gone were the days when you had to carry around binders and papers! It also meant that he received all changes and updates automatically and electronically. It was good to be able to focus on what needed to be done and not on sorting out piles of paper.

The DMAIC approach to continuous process improvement helps to ensure that projects deliver maximum financial benefits to the business. Teams achieve this through a systematic and analytical approach to problem identification, solution development and sustainable solution implementation. When the DMAIC process is complete process

SMART QUOTES

People will pay more to be entertained than educated.

Johnny Carson

Can Six Sigma be used outside manufacturing?

Six Sigma started in manufacturing but has spread to many other processes, functions and disciplines. Most industries have now undertaken some form of Six Sigma project. Good process analysis, at an early stage, is key to understanding why Six Sigma techniques will be appropriate. Six Sigma used in non-manufacturing projects is often described as transactional Six Sigma, e.g. invoicing processes exist in both service and manufacturing industries and have been the subject of Six Sigma projects in both types of business.

improvements are handed over to process owners, lessons learned are recorded and shared and the project team is recognized and rewarded for its successful efforts.

The principles of the DMAIC process

Success in a Six Sigma project team depends on the members of the team operating to the same values and working with a set of principles established by experienced successful Six Sigma Black Belts and companies that have operated in Six Sigma mode for long periods of time. Here are the principles:

1. Continuous improvement activities require a simple but systematic project methodology.

2. Continuous improvement activities can make significant use of Six Sigma analytical techniques.

3. The best project process for continuous improvement is DMAIC: Define – Measure & Analyse – Improve – Control.

4. All continuous improvement projects must develop and agree a Project Charter early in the Define phase.

5. All analytical tools and data are linked to the DMAIC project and held in single project data repository.

6. Checklists are used to set the targets for each phase and to monitor and record the achievement of targets.

7. At the end of each phase, a completed checklist and project sponsor approval must be achieved before funding and resources can be released for the next phase.

8. All team members should be rewarded on the basis of team and individual targets.

9. Projects that fail to meet agreed targets, in any phase, will be stopped by their project sponsor or returned to the Define phase for redefinition of their Project Charter.

The DMAIC project methodology

There are five distinct phases in a DMAIC project, each one with a number of key activities that are completed before the next phase can be started.

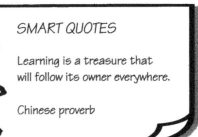

SMART QUOTES

Learning is a treasure that
will follow its owner everywhere.

Chinese proverb

Define

This is where the Six Sigma team defines what the project is trying to achieve in practical and very specific terms. Project definition is an absolutely critical activity where success or failure can be built into a project. Successful definition is vital to building a high probability of success and learning into all continuous improvement projects.

All projects must develop and agree a Project Charter – a two-page statement that summarizes the key logistics and framework of the project. At the end of Define, the project team should have a very clear view of how they will be successful on this improvement project by producing the following documents:

- Project Charter

- Problem/Opportunity Statement

- Process Requirements

- Stakeholder and Barrier to Change Analysis

- Project Risk Summary

- Team Targets and Training

At the end of Define, the project team knows about the effects of problems and customer requirements for changes.

Measure & Analyse

The team identifies the measurements it will use to test possible causes and carry out quantitative and qualitative analysis. The Measure & Analyse phases have been combined into a single phase because of the interrelated nature of the two phases (some Black Belts like to keep these phases separate).

One of the key differences that Six Sigma brings to projects is the rigour of good data and effective use of analytical techniques. It is important that project teams are working with the right data and using the best quantitative and qualitative analysis tools.

The presentation of insights and conclusions from the Measure & Ana-

SMART
ANSWERS
TO TOUGH
QUESTIONS

lyse phase is also a critical component in building management acceptance and support for improvement plans.

The Measure phase has the following outputs:

- Key Questions and Data Slicing

- Data Collection Sheets

- Data Definitions and Sampling

- Baselines and Performance Indicators

- Best Practices and Benchmarks

While the Analyse phase concentrates on these issues:

- Analysis Tool Selection

- Data Collection and Analysis Files

- Root Cause Analysis

- Analysis Conclusions

- Initial Cost–Benefit Analysis

What are the best analytical tools to use for Six Sigma?

There are a variety of analytical tools available to support Six Sigma projects. Some of the most popular tools for statistical analysis include Minitab and Statgraphics. Microsoft Excel is generally more widely used and available. It provides adequate basic functionality for most requirements. Advanced Statistical tools can be turned on within Excel to provide support for most basic quantitative analysis. Minitab is often seen to be the most logical choice by Six Sigma training companies. Project teams need to decide their approach given the trade off between Minitab's advanced statistical power and Excel's wider availability.

It is very important to make the right decision on which analytical tools to use in given circumstances. A good place to start is to look at the tool selection matrix in the Measure & Analyse chapter. This matrix is designed to help you to select the right types of analysis tools depending on the business problem. In addition, there are good examples in training materials and in the Blue Computers' case. The key is often to find a similar project or problem and to select analysis tools that have been shown to be effective in helping project teams to solve problems. It is also important to remember that you do not need to use all the analysis tools to solve a problem, just the ones that give real insights. If you have outstanding concerns about which analysis tools you may have to consult a Black Belt or talk to an expert in a specific topic area.

Improve

Once the team has discovered the root cause or causes of the problem or opportunity, it generates a series of potential solutions. They then use various techniques to identify the best one. The improve phase is not complete until the team has run a pilot and confirmed that the solution does deliver the expected benefits. Because of the care taken in the Measure & Analyse phases, the team can measure the delivery of financial as well as qualitative benefits. Here are the steps in this part of the process:

- Solution Filter

- Pilot

- Solution Definition and Business Case

- Solution Risk Summary

This phase focuses on the improvement opportunities identified in the Measure & Analyse phases. The team filters suggested solutions and runs pilots until they are certain of their preferred solution because they have seen its impact. The business case for change is built and risks are assessed. At the end of Improve, the new process solution is ready for implementation.

Control

In the control phase the project team hands over the new process to the person or team responsible for ongoing management of the process. Once again there are financial and other measures in place to ensure that the new process is working in a way that ensures the organization realizes the benefits from it.

> SMART QUOTES
>
> Knowledge is of two kinds: We know a subject ourselves, or we know where we can find information about it.
>
> Samuel Johnson

The control phase involves the implementation and handover of the solution identified in Improve. It is important to sustain the improved process, to build employee acceptance and to handover the solution to the process owner. At the end of Control, the project team should record lessons learned, ensure there is an agreed process scorecard for ongoing performance management and that good project team performance is recognized and rewarded. The steps are:

- Ongoing Process Management

We asked a number of experienced Black Belts three questions. This is what one Black Belt, Michael Jacobsen, told us:

What went well?

The teams worked very hard to make the right decisions and improve their processes. We used small tasks at first to win some credibility with the front line workers. The use of benchmarking was a great tool for our team. By sharing information through events with GE and Boeing I was able to work with other industries and learn from their knowledge.

What didn't go well?

Lack of reliable data. Lack of commitment from management. No reward for team efforts. The change must be made a requirement to make the social change and in my old company that was not done.

What would you do differently?

Require management to be certified as Green or Black Belts. Make management the first wave with personnel on the floor. Make rewards for the teams that are not tied to total savings. By tying the reward to savings we may generate a competitive not co-operative environment. Integrate the project management and software training with the Six Sigma training. Do not use computers for the first two weeks of training.

- Process Improvements and Control

- Lessons Learned

As at the end of each phase, there is a multi-topic checklist for the project manager to complete.

Activities and outputs

In each phase of the DMAIC process there is a set of activities that project teams need to complete in order to gain approval for phase completion and for the next phase to begin. At the end of each phase there is a checklist of key deliverables that must be completed to the satisfaction of both the project manager and the project sponsor. The checklists set the required achievement level for each phase, so that the project team can understand what needs to be achieved and by when. The successful management and completion of these checklists defines the relationship between the project manager and project sponsor. Experienced project managers and sponsors have contributed to ensuring that the checklists are fair and stretching challenges of the effective management and completion of key project tasks. The checklists are key mechanisms for ensuring that financial benefits are identified, secured and delivered as rapidly as possible by the project team.

Timescales

The average DMAIC project will last 3–6 months depending on the complexity of the business problem or the solution implementation. The timeline is also dependent on the amount of data and whether it is readily available. If new data collection is required, the project may take longer depending on the time period over which new data is generated, recorded and collected.

Dave Spencer smiled. He was now going to get the chance he had been looking for. He was confident that he now had the right project, right team and the right processes to be successful. He still needed to build a relationship with his project sponsor but that would take time.

Dave felt that the Six Sigma opportunity was working for him. Many colleagues were now asking him questions about what a Black Belt did and how tough was the training. Places on Black Belt training were hard

What will make Six Sigma stick in our company?

One of the key challenges for any new improvement programme is whether it can be made to stick in the company. For Six Sigma it is critical that senior management are seen to display strong sponsorship. Black Belts and Green Belts need to be trained quickly and with minimum interference with the ongoing business. The Six Sigma programme must be presented in a way that engages the support of the broader firm. The organization must be prepared to shift from a culture that is often one of "fire fighting" to planning, measurement and delivery. Six Sigma must balance the needs of multiple stakeholders if it is to be successful.

to secure and Dave was pleased that he had got trained early. He had also attended an evening workshop where he had met other Black Belts from different companies. They were at all stages of DMAIC projects but Dave had picked up some useful advice and tips on project management. He was surprised how open the Black Belts were with each other about best practices in Six Sigma. He had enjoyed his first encounter with a new network of people who thought and behaved in a new way. "It was a really positive and optimistic meeting. Six Sigma really is a ticket to a new way of working" – he told the project team at the weekly meeting.

2

The DMAIC Define
Phase and Charter

There is an old Chinese proverb which says that every journey starts with a first step. The Define phase is the first step in Six Sigma. It is the time when the project team design success into their Six Sigma project.

A DMAIC project always starts with a Define phase and a Project Charter. The Define phase is focused on getting the project properly set up so that it can deliver real value. There is an old army saying that states "Time spent in reconnaissance is rarely wasted." It is the same for the Define phase "Time spent setting up your project is rarely wasted." This is for two reasons: firstly you need to ensure that the project is right, and secondly you need to spend time getting the team working together. Fact-based analysis is very important, but so is a well prepared and effective project team.

During the Define phase the project team will produce a number of key outputs:

- A Project Charter including problem statement, the goal statement/objectives, scope, key project milestones and initial financial targets

- A project plan and people resource requirements

- Voice of the customer (VOC) and critical to quality (CTQ) analysis (as seen earlier in our introduction)

The project team will work on a number of different activities to build up the Project Charter and plans. These include:

- Problem/Opportunity statement

- Process maps, SIPOC (Supplier Input Process Output Customer) and insights on processes/quick wins

- Stakeholder and Barrier to Change Analysis

- Project Risk Summary

- Team Targets and Training

The team will also have the opportunity to use a number of qualitative analysis tools (see the appendices). Typically these will include process mapping, SIPOC, analysis of customer surveys and brainstorming.

By the end of the Define phase the project team is set up to be successful – it has not yet tried to solve the problem!

The Project Charter

The Project Charter provides the focus for the project team as well as the means for senior management to be sure that the project remains relevant to the business and that it is making sensible progress. It is the expected performance contract between the project team and management. In effect the Project Charter says, "If you give us these resources, we will give you these benefits."

Some Black Belts like to have a dynamic Project Charter that develops with the overall project. Others see it as a discrete document that is completed at the beginning of a project and then purely used for reference. We favour the dynamic Project Charter approach (however, this does not mean that team members can change target dates and benefits without seeking approval!). The Project Charter also helps to define the relationship between the project team, Black Belt and project sponsor.

The Charter contains a number of standard areas:

- A description of the project

- A problem/opportunity statement (derived from a customer perspective)

- A goal statement

- Outline financials

- Target dates

- Scope (both in scope and out of scope activities)

- Risk summary

- Linkage between the project and overall business imperatives

- Team names, roles, resourcing and contribution

SMART is a useful acronym for the Project Charter – targets should be Stretching, Measurable, Achievable, Related to the customer and Time targeted.

What do I need to put in a Project Charter?

What is the project name?

Who is the person that has agreed to support this project as the project sponsor?

Who is the person that has been assigned as the project manager for this project?

What is the reference number for this project?

What is a summary of the problem/opportunity?

What is the overall goal that is to be achieved by this project?

What are the costs and benefits?

What are the estimated investment costs for this project?

What will be the additional costs incurred from putting the new process in place?

What are the financial benefits that will come from the new process?

All of these numbers will emerge over time as the project comes to its conclusions

What are the initial expectations?

What are the expectations of costs and benefits when the project begins? (High-level estimates)

What is the business case?

The team will only be in a position to complete this box when they have completed the business case in the Measure & Analyse stage

What are the expected customer impact and intangible benefits?

Note: This also will build and change during the Measure & Analyse phase

What are the project dates?

What is included in the project scope?

Consider answering who, what where and when to clearly cover all relevant aspects of the project

What is excluded from the project scope?

Consider the same questions who, what, where and when

What is a summary of the project risks?

What business imperatives are impacted?

What impact does the project have?

This should be stated as specific and quantifiable improvements

Who are team members, what is their role and in what phases of DMAIC will they be involved and when?

The role of knowledge manager must be assigned to one of the team members

What percentage of each team members' time will be on the project, and what are their Six Sigma qualifications – Black Belt (BB) Green Belt (GB)?

Dave Spencer cast his eye over the Project Charter (see Figure 2.1) that came out of the first team meeting. He recognized that it was a good first pass and that it would get better as the project progressed. He sent off an email to his project sponsor asking him to sign off electronically that he agreed with the charter.

To quote Mr Fukuhara, you've got to "pick up the pencil." You can talk and talk and talk about it, but until you actually start defining the voice of the customer and creating a chart, it's all talk. You don't have to do things perfectly – there's a lot of benefit from just making an attempt.

Robert H. Schaefer, Reliability Engineering Director, Product Assurance and Validation, Chevrolet-Pontiac-Canada Group, General Motors Corp.

Project name	Project sponsor	Project manager	Reference
Delivery & Predictability Performance	John Kelly	Dave Spencer	D&P/002

Summary of problem/opportunity	
1	Blue Computers needs to improve on-time delivery from current 60–70% to better than 95%.
2	Blue Computers have an opportunity to significantly improve customer satisfaction through predictable delivery performance. This will enable the customer to more effectively plan systems' downtime and installation/upgrade resources
3	Blue Computers will, by fixing the delivery predictability issues, enhance the cashflow position of the Company and therefore overall profitability. Late and inaccurate deliveries impact invoicing and payment cycles; currently "cash-to-cash" cycle time is 60 days, we need this to be below 50 days by Sep 01 and below 40 days by Dec 01

Objective/goal statement	
Goal statement	To increase the percentage of customer deliveries arriving on-time and in line with prediction/commitment made by Sales. Current performance of 60% on-time to be improved to better than 95% by Sept 2001.

Cost/benefit	Initial expectations	Business case	S	Comments
Capital costs	300,000		G	Software & hardware upgrade
Operating costs	450,000		G	Training and education programme, ongoing monitoring.
Operating benefits	800,000		G	Better business flow, higher Customer Satisfaction, better revenue linearity

Figure 2.1 Blue Computers Project Charter

Cost–benefit Total	50,000			G		

Expected customer impact/intangible benefits	
1	Delivery on-time performance at 95% or better. Will enable customer to plan systems' downtime and resources for installation or system upgrade.
2	Achieve commitments/promises; to raise the credibility of Blue Computers and enhance reputation as a corporation that "keeps it's promises"
3	Faster cycle time on sales orders from receipt of order to delivery of Blue product. Will satisfy customer receipt requirements and Blue Computer's need for an efficient operation.
4	Improved service level and customer satisfaction: customer receives product in good time and when planned.

Project dates	Start	Target	S	Actual	Comments
Authorization				01-Jan	
Define	01-Jan	31-Jan	G	07-Feb	1 week slippage, authorizing manager off-site
Measure & Analyse	01-Feb	28-Feb	G	01-Mar	On schedule
Improve	01-Mar	31-Mar	G	13-Apr	2 weeks slippage, improvement proposals' costs re-examined
Control	01-Apr	30-Apr	G	08-May	1 week slippage, no issue

	Project scope – included	Project scope - excluded
1	All shipments from UK manufacturing & German hub direct to EMEA end-users or resellers	All shipments from resellers on to end-users
2	All third party items merged prior to delivery	All non-EMEA shipments

	Risk summary	Comments
1	Medium	If areas of concern addressed rapidly, will migrate to "low risk"
2	Sales organization will not adopt changes	Need to work with Sales Director on this one
3	Most obvious solutions will have a high capital cost	Cannot really comment until we have a set of solutions
4	Project will not deliver adequate improvement	Need to verify expected performance improvement, also establish "Voice of Customer" input

	Business imperatives impacted	Project impact
1	Delivery predictability	Improve from 68% to over 95%
2	Delivery performance	Improve from 60% On Time Delivery (OTD) to over 95% OTD
3	Cash to cash cycle time	Improve average from 60 days to 42 days

	Team members	Role & phases	%	Q	Start date	
1	Dave Spencer	Team leader: All phases	100	BB	01-Jan-01	30-Jun-01
2	Grant Stevens	Content Expert – Delivery metrics and analysis: All phases	100		01-Jan-01	30-Apr-01
3	Dave Brown	Content Expert – Sales: All phases	100		01-Jan-01	30-Jun-01
4	Nancy Hardman	Content Expert – Third party/Supplier management: All phases	50	GB	01-Jan-01	30-Apr-01
5	John Sheridan	Content Expert – Quality Engineer: All phases	100		01-Jan-01	30-Jun-01
6	Johann Schmidt	Content Expert – Order Processing: All phases	100	GB	01-Jan-01	30-Apr-01
7	Kath Taylor	Content Expert – Finance: Analysis & Control phases	30		01-Feb-01	30-Apr-01

Project plan

The project plan is a key document which sets out the target start and end dates of each phase of the project. It is usually created in an Excel spreadsheet or Microsoft Project plan. The highlights of the project plan are summarized in the Project Charter. The main project plan can be attached as a separate and much more detailed plan.

A typical project plan contains a logical information including answers to the following questions:

- What activity is required in each phase?

- What group/group of activities does it fit within (e.g. a phase or an output)?

- How long will the activity take? (e.g. how many mandays?)

- When will it start and finish?

- Who is responsible? Who will actually do the work?

- What are the critical dependencies? (e.g. what needs to happen before and after this activity?)

Dave used a project plan template designed for DMAIC to build his project plan quickly. He knew that he could use Microsoft Project or Excel for the plan. He chose Excel because he knew that many of his team had not yet got MS Project on their computers.

Define – getting to the Project Charter and working smartly

Now, what do you have to do to get to a strong Project Charter? Six

Project Plan
Blue Computer Ltd

Delivery and Predictability Sx Sigma Project.
DMAIC

Key
Management review
Team - planned duration
Team - actual duration

O Activity start
X Activity stop

Project Plan

Activity	Responsible	Oct'00	Nov'00	Dec'00	Jan'01 week 1	Jan'01 week 2	Jan'01 week 3	Jan'01 week 4	Jan'01 week 5	Feb'01 week 6	Feb'01 week 7	Feb'01 week 8	Feb'01 week 9
Define need	WD, AB, HP, HS												
Senior Management review	WD, AB, HP, HS												
Select Champion / sponsor	HP, HS												
Determine Methodology / Approach	HP, HS												
Initial Scoping	HP, HS												
ROI	HP, HS												
Authorization	WD, AB, HP, HS												
Select Team Lead & Members	HP, HS												
Identify Team Training Requirements	HP, HS												
Deliver Team Training	HP, HS												
Team Kick-off	WD, AB, HP, HS												
Define Phase - target	DS & Team												
Define Phase - actual	DS & Team												
Phase - Exit	DS & Team												
Measure & Analyze Phase - target	DS & Team												
Measure & Analyze Phase - actual	DS & Team												
Phase - Exit	DS & Team												
Improve Phase - target	DS & Team												
Improve Phase - actual	DS & Team												
Phase - Exit	DS & Team												
Control Phase - target	DS & Team												
Control Phase - actual	DS & Team												
Phase - Exit	DS & Team												
Final Sign-off	WD, AB, HP, HS												
Ongoing Monitoring	DS, GS, JS												

Figure 2.2 *Dave Spencer's project plan*

Sigma projects require a fair amount of documentation to show both how the project team has undertaken fact-based analysis and to allow knowledge sharing. But, of course, Six Sigma is not just the preparation of the documents and templates. The objective is to deliver financial benefits by implementing new solutions effectively as quickly as possible. The project team should always look for opportunities to reduce the effort required by working smartly and assigning project tasks to the most appropriate people (based on their ability and time available).

As we mentioned at the beginning of the chapter, a number of activities and outputs are required in the Define phase to support the development of the Project Charter. In this section, we will take you through how to develop these outputs and how they fit with the Project Charter:

- Problem/Opportunity Statement

- Process maps, SIPOC (Supplier Input Process Output Customer) and insights on processes/quick wins

- Stakeholder and Barrier to Change Analysis

- Project Risk Summary

- Team Targets and Training

Let us start then with the first step towards identifying what the problem or opportunity is, and where the business case might lie to justify the setting up of a Six Sigma project.

Creating a good Problem/Opportunity Statement

In the introduction we saw how Dave Spencer documented the first part of the define phase – the voice of the customer (VOC). We now move to the next question – the Problem/Opportunity Statement worked out by

Who should I have on my team?

There are a number of standard ways of organizing a Six Sigma project. The team will consist of at least one Black Belt and several Green Belts. Some of the project team may be undergoing training and this must then be managed so that there are not too many trainees on one project. Master Black Belts can be used for very complex statistical analysis, project team coaching and quality assurance. Six Sigma projects always start with a Define phase. This phase is critical and it is essential that a project team develop a good Project Charter.

Scottish Black Belt

the project team with the voice of the customer at the front of their minds. The questions are:

• *What is the problem or area of concern?*

This defines the process areas that the project will address.

• *What impact does it have? Why is it a problem?*

This is the 'so what?' test. A problem or an opportunity statement is only valid if it is backed up with a statement of its impact on the business. The answer to this question will become clearer as the project progresses.

• *What evidence do you have?*

Even at this early stage you are asked to give specific evidence of the impact. This will probably start off with anecdotal data from customers, suppliers and employees. As the project progresses, the team can refine their evidence during the Measure & Analyse phases.

• *What is the implication of not fixing the problem?*

Where the previous question talks about current evidence for change, this question looks at the "do nothing" possibility. If the problem or opportunity is important enough, the implications for not fixing it could be very serious.

The responses to these questions can now be summarized into a small number of connected statements. The team now has a high level statement of what the project is about including good pointers as to the likely shape of an outline cost–benefit case.

Summary of problem/opportunity	
1	
2	
3	
4	

Figure 2.3a Problem/Opportunity Statement

Dave was pleased with the Problem/Opportunity Statement that his team developed (see Figure 2.3b). He felt that it set out a compelling reason for change.

Understanding the key processes and insights

It is important that the project team should define early on in the project the processes that it is looking at. This allows the team to focus on specific process improvement opportunities. As part of the Define phase the project team should use a SIPOC analysis to define the high-level view of the processes.

Problem/opportunity statement	
What is the problem/ area of concern?	Deliveries from Blue Computers into EMEA are only arriving on-time for two-thirds (60%) of shipments.
Why is this a problem and what impact does it have?	The customer has to bring down their IT systems to install Blue products. If deliveries are late, then customer's system downtime is extended awaiting Blue deliveries. If early, then temporary storage of hardware is an issue.
What evidence do you have?	Blue Computer's own metrics plus customer feedback via sales offices indicate an on-time delivery performance of 60% with a late of 28% and an early of 12%.
What is the implication of not fixing the problem?	Customers will migrate to other suppliers of computer and network systems in order to ensure minimum downtime during any given IT upgrade: i.e. loss of market share for Blue Computers.
Summary of problem/opportunity	
1	Blue Computers needs to improve on-time delivery from current 60–70% to better than 95%.
2	Blue Computers have an opportunity to significantly improve customer satisfaction through predictable delivery performance. This will enable the customer to more effectively plan systems' downtime and installation/upgrade resources.
3	Blue Computers will, by fixing the delivery predictability issues, enhance the cashflow position of the company and therefore overall profitability. Late and inaccurate deliveries impact invoicing and payment cycles; currently "cash-to-cash" cycle time is 60 days, we need this to be below 50 days by Sep-01 and below 40 days by Dec-01.

Figure 2.3b Problem/Opportunity Statement

SIPOC insights and implications

SIPOC stands for Supplier – Input – Process – Output – Customer. SIPOC is a qualitative analytical tool that is designed to focus a project team's attention on the key activities involved in a process that flows between a company, its customers and suppliers. It is a high-level process flowchart that focuses the team's attention on the key processes that require improvement. The output from a SIPOC diagram should be a list of key insights and implications. The implications should state these in a way that leads on to an understanding of problems and opportunities. Dave's team quickly developed their outline SIPOC and process map (see Figure 2.4)

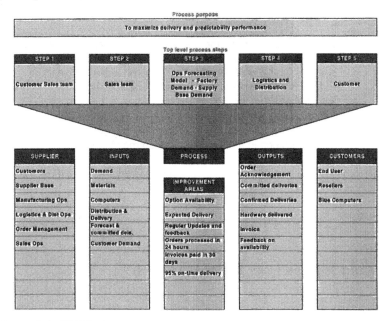

Figure 2.4 SIPOC chart

The SIPOC can be used in combination with more detailed process maps to focus the team's attention on the critical processes, flows and performance indicators. The real value of the SIPOC and process maps is in extracting the insights and in understanding their implications.

	Key SIPOC insights	Project implications
1	The process actually starts and ends with the customer	Customer is also one of the suppliers, not always apparent from process operation
2	Feedback/confirmation of delivery commit comes very late in the process around third stage of planning process – average 8 days from receipt of order to confirmation of delivery	Process revamp will also be required, now or later
3	Sales team have two customers, the end-user and the forecasting process; they do not treat internal customer with same due diligence as external customer	Sales team need to be central to this project, need to see them-selves as part of the solution from day 1
4	Distribution Operations may not be the issue as the delays come from earlier steps in the process than Distribution Operations	Problem and resolution may lie out with the delivery operation, which may be why previous attempts at rectifying this issue have been unsuccessful

Figure 2.5 SIPOC insights

Lessons learned from previous projects

Smart project managers understand the term SWAG – "Stolen With Glee". They know that there is a good chance on a Six Sigma project that someone else will have done something similar in the past. They are masters of re-use. Senior project managers and their directors like re-use, they get more value from the past and they get to see best practice knowledge spreading through the project managers and their teams. It is always disappointing to see the opposite effect when one project manager learns very little from his colleagues. In the Define phase, the Six Sigma approach should make sure that project teams actively look for previous projects from which they can learn. Best project practices should be available electronically so that teams can learn from the earlier Six Sigma projects.

Dave's team had struggled, at the start, to find information from other projects. However, Dave had been good at tracking down other Black Belts from his training course and they had contributed some great insights. Dave got the team to brainstorm what they would now do differently. He made sure it was built into the project plan and templates.

Show me how your project team has learned lessons from previous projects?

It is important that the project team actively seeks to learn from past experiences and projects, so:

- What are the key lessons that improve our knowledge of this problem or opportunity area?
- What is the source of this data?
- How will the lessons learned be included on this project?

KILLER QUESTIONS

	Lessons learned from previous projects	Source	Project implications
1	Tinkering with the forecasting process has not fixed this issue	Previous project on forecast process	New project will incorporate the forecasting process along with all other aspects
2	Adjusting the internal metrics to give a better picture simply masks the true extent of the problem	Metrics revised on multiple occasions – issue unresolved	New metrics will be required but these *must* reflect actual customer experience
3	No fix will work unless it encompasses the sales and order entry functions as well as Operations	Previous projects within Operations	Sales function will be represented on project team to ensure the right scope
4	Senior management sponsorship at the outset will better enable the team and add legitimacy to the project	Previous projects in Operations	Senior management public kick-off and active sponsor are essential to success

Figure 2.6 Lessons learned

Existing sources of data

We have said that Six Sigma describes a set of data-driven tools and methodologies designed to significantly improve the quality of products and services delivered to customers. In the Measure & Analyse phases, we will take this much further, but at this point the team should look for existing data that can help the project

Data availability and time periods

Data availability will have a significant impact on the ability of the project team to develop the project recommendations and to persuade management to implement their conclusions. The team should try to assess, early in the project, how much good quality data is already available and what data will need to be collected from scratch. The validity and usefulness of statistical data also depends on its time period. Data

gathered over a longer period of time has more validity than data gathered over a short period. Data with a short period of coverage may be useful where there is significant variation in performance.

Data type and quantity of data

Similarly, we need to note the type of data and its collection method to evaluate its value. For example, if all customers have input to a satisfaction measure whenever they place an order, we may place more value on this data compared to the occasional example of verbal feedback coming from one customer via a salesperson.

SMART
ANSWERS
TO TOUGH
QUESTIONS

What is the best way to re-use existing data

- What sources of data can you use for this project? It is important that the project team knows about and makes best use of data that already exists before requesting new data.
- What time period does the data cover, e.g. last 6 months, and how current is the data?
- What sort of data is this? For example, spreadsheet, hard copy, report, customer surveys.
- How much data is there? For example, daily or hourly measures, size of files, number of lines/measures.

The team now has good insights on where the project fits in the process between its suppliers and customers. It has learned lessons from previous projects and taken its first look at existing sources of data that it will use in the Measure & Analyse phases. Figure 2.7 shows what Dave's team concluded about data availability for their project.

	Existing sources of data	Time period	Data type	Quantity of data
1	Customer feedback through sales and order entry functions	Last 3 months	Customer-satisfaction data entries by order entry (OE) function	All customers who have responded
2	Blue Computers' delivery and predictability metrics (ORACLE)	Last quarter	Internal metrics/ORACLE based	All shipments into EMEA
3	Anecdotal evidence from recent customer visit to Operations in the UK	Dec-00	Verbal during feedback sessions	One key customer

Figure 2.7 Data availability and re-use

Stakeholder and barriers to change analysis

Stakeholders are individuals or groups that have a direct influence on the success of the project and its implementation. Stakeholder interest in a project will be driven by their perception of how it will impact their work. Projects are too often blind-sided by a new stakeholder coming to light half way through the project or, even worse, towards the end of the project. This is particularly true of process change projects where there are many people affected across multiple locations. It is vitally important that the team recognizes all stakeholders as early in the project as possible. You may have a stakeholder who is very much against the changes envisaged by the project. The team must monitor the effectiveness of their communication with this stakeholder and their acceptance

SMART VOICES

A communication plan is important in order to involve the personnel with the Six Sigma initiative by showing them how it works, how it is related to their jobs and the benefits from it. By doing this, resistance to change can be reduced.

K. Henderson and J. Evans, "Successful implementation of Six Sigma" (2000).

of the team's conclusions. A good question to ask your project sponsor is what he/she can do to help to manage negative stakeholders

The project team needs to understand likely barriers to change and what can be done to reduce them. The DMAIC process encourages the team to identify these early on.

Different stakeholders will have different needs. A financial controller will need a lot of information but mainly related to financials. A senior director of the company may need surprisingly little information but can have a huge impact if the project team is seen as threatening to areas under his or her control. There is a tendency for project teams to manage stakeholder communications in bursts. This can lead to breakdowns in relations between project teams and neglected stakeholders. The aim of the stakeholder analysis and action plans is to make communications consistent and effective.

Six Sigma projects often use RAG status indicators (a simple red, amber, green signal on project effectiveness). The RAG status box is also useful in designing reports. Many managers may only want to know red and amber items. If you have stakeholders with a red status, don't ignore them – make sure that you address their issues. If you don't they will not go away.

The earlier the team thinks about barriers to change, the more likely it is to identify the actions that will tackle the problem area and reduce the

How to analyse Stakeholders?

- Who are the key individuals or groups that are either impacted by the project or need to be involved in one way or another?

Expected impact

- What is the expected impact that each individual or group could have on the successful completion of the project?
  Use a scale of 1–5 where (1 = minor impact on project activities only to 5 = major impact, e.g. could stop the project proceeding or achieving project objectives)

- What viewpoint/attitude does each stakeholder have about the project?
  Use a scale of –5 to +5 where (–5 = strongly resistant and needs to be managed carefully, 0 = neutral, +5 = strongly supportive and can be used to drive activities)

- What is the relationship of each stakeholder to the project?
  Think about the following:
  - Is impacted by the outcome
  - Can influence the outcome
  - Has expertise and key information
  - Has decision authority
  - Provides budget or resource

- What is the best way to communicate with each stakeholder?
  Consider the following:
  - Meet with regularly
  - Invite to team meetings
  - Meet informally when required
  - Send copy of project and meeting reports

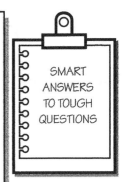

SMART
ANSWERS
TO TOUGH
QUESTIONS

barrier. Most project teams can tell you very quickly what the main barriers to change will be.

Dave's team at Blue Computers has now looked at the stakeholders and

Which way is your company headed – towards spectacular results with Six Sigma or down the road to another management fad? How to see the signs that Six Sigma is becoming disconnected from the core business:

- Downward trends in deployment and results indicators
- Flagging support for Six Sigma projects
- Evidence of Six Sigma isolation
- A failure to apply basic improvement principles to Six Sigma deployment
- A gradual blurring of Six Sigma roles and responsibilities.

Max Isaac and Anton McBurnie, "Troubled times for Six Sigma", taken from Six Sigma Exchange Newsletter (July 2002), vol. 2, issue 7, pp. 2–3.

barriers to change. They now have a much clearer idea about the people involved in the project and understood the potential threats to a successful implementation.

It is also good practice to document your key assumptions (Figure 2.9) in a project. By doing this you make clear the principles and environment that you are working under in the project. If these assumptions change significantly (because, for example, of a new strategic plan or an acquisition) the project team should revisit the Project Charter to ensure that it is still relevant. Assumptions may well include, for example, such areas as business conditions, data availability, access to customers and sites. This part of the Define phase may give the project team some hard choices. They must face up to the barriers that people and outside influencers might put in the way of the project. It is much better to identify a barrier to change that is a "show stopper" now rather than later. Be open, be honest and above all be clear that this is the right project for your company.

	Stakeholders	I	±	Relationship to project	Communication plan	S
1	William Doors (II)	5	3	EMEA Operations Director, provides resource and will be final owner of new process	Monthly status meetings and copied on project executive review	G
2	Anders Berndts	3	0	EMEA Transportation & Distribution Manager, part of EMEA logistics division	Weekly status meetings, copied on weekly project meeting minutes	G
3	Harry Palmer	4	0	Sales Director, responsible for EMEA customer-care. Needs the process to work flawlessly	Weekly status meetings, copied on weekly project meeting minutes	A
4	Hannibal Speaker	4	2	Logistics Director, responsible for process ownership, the metrics are his	Weekly status meetings, copied on weekly project meeting minutes	G

	Barriers to change (BtoC)	Project implications	Solution	S
1	New product introduction activities may consume resources	Cannot get the right team membership	Determine outlook on NPI and assign other resources to cover	A
2	Same model in USA & Asia/Pacific	Corporate inertia = failure to authorize project	Sell the solution to corporate	A
3	Long-term benefits outweighed by short-term costs	Funding unavailable	Conduct robust ROI with demonstrable payback	A
4	Availability of team members	Cannot get the right team membership	Determine "ideal team" and approach line managers for support	G
5	Availability of training resources	Cannot get the team trained to the necessary skill-level	Discuss situation with HR & training functions	G

Figure 2.8 Stakeholders and barriers to change

| 6 | Existing process embedded in organization | Process owners won't adopt the new practices | Involve process owner management in Define and Measure phases | A |
| 7 | Risk to existing customers while we "get well" | Unwillingness to change customer interface processes unless transparent or demonstrably positive for the customer | Involve process owner management in Define and Measure phases | A |

Figure 2.8 *Continued*

	Key project assumptions	Implications
1	Issues can be resolved in the stated 3–6 month period	If the project overruns momentum for change could be lost
2	All the required skills are available within Blue Computers' staff	If all the skills are not available need to consider seconding staff from other regions or bringing in third parties (consultants)
3	ROI will support project cost-base	If ROI does not justify project, customer dissatisfaction may become "acceptable" to organization
4	Project will be authorized at local and corporate level	Project will not start if authorization is not forthcoming
5	Any changes made will have only positive impact on customer experience	Customer will not want to see something else deteriorate to "pay for" the improvement in delivery/predictability

Figure 2.9 *Project assumptions*

Project risk summary

All good project managers are good risk managers. They accept that there are always risks on projects, they understand those risks and they actively manage them. There are two benefits of acknowledging the risks involved in any project. Firstly, you need to know whether the risks involved outweigh the potential benefits of a project. Secondly, early risk detection provides the opportunity to manage and mitigate it through the project. The purpose of risk analysis is to be proactive in listing the risks and to have a plan for managing the main ones.

Why do Six Sigma projects sometimes fail?

Six Sigma projects can fail for all the same reasons that most projects fail. Typical issues to watch out for are lack of senior management leadership, lack of acceptance by the business, poorly executed project processes, lack of resources (particularly time from part time team members) and lack of focus on project financial benefits. Project managers are key to success and to managing the risks inherent in projects. Project managers grow in experience over time and it is important that companies should be constantly developing project management skills through small projects so that there is a strong pool of good project managers available in a company.

SMART
ANSWERS
TO TOUGH
QUESTIONS

Risk can be summarized into a simple table (Figure 2.10a) where "Prob" is the probability a risk will happen and "Imp" is its impact. The use of probability and impact helps to differentiate major risks (e.g. high prob-

	Project risks	Prob	Imp	Preventive/contingent action	S
A					
B					
C					

Figure 2.10a Risk summary outline

ability, high impact) from lower risk issues (e.g. low probability/low impact).

Dave Spencer asked his team to identify the risks, their probability and impact and then to identify action plans to deal with them. The team then assessed the status of each risk, as either red (immediate action is required) amber, (future action is probably going to be required) or green (where no action is required either because the probability of it occurring is low or because the impact is low). The project team liked the red, amber and green approach, it was a simple and effective way to get the message across (see Figure 2.10b).

It soon became clear to the team that the major risk they needed to manage was their relationship with the sales organization. One of the team smiled at Dave and said "I think you are going to need a lot of help from the project sponsor with that Dave." The team summarized their risk analysis for inclusion in the Project Charter. Dave Spencer decided to

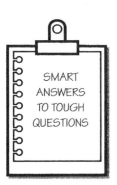

SMART
ANSWERS
TO TOUGH
QUESTIONS

Why do I need a project sponsor?

Great project sponsors know how to ask the right questions and when they are needed to ensure the success of projects. The role of the project sponsor is to champion a project, to promote the project to the wider business and to ensure that it remains on track. The role of the sponsor is not to do the project, however interesting. Great project sponsors know how to spend the right amount of time with the project manager and team. They are usually very good at picking out the difficult questions that no one has covered but which represents a significant problem or opportunity for the project. Great project sponsors are not inactive or absent. They somehow know when they are required and the difference between sponsorship and interference. Good project sponsors are like an umbrella protecting their project managers and teams.

Project risks	P	I	Preventive/contingent action	
A	Most obvious solutions will have a high capital cost	5	7	Make low capital cost one of the solution selection criteria	A
B	Timescale will not allow project completion	2	3	Verify expected timescale, discuss contingencies with management, add flex to timescale on project plan	G
C	Sales organization will not adopt changes	6	9	Lobby sales organization to ensure they are part of the process from day 1	R
D	Customers will not accept changed conditions	1	4	Should be invisible to customers	G
E	Project will not deliver adequate improvement	4	7	Verify scope of project and expected deliverables, highlight issues to senior management	A
F	ROI will not meet corporate requirements on payback	1	7	Re-evaluate ROI, ensure buy-in from corporate finance officers	G
G	Cost overrun	4	3	Establish flexibility built into cost limits, re-evaluate ROI and Project Plan to ensure calibration	G
H	Team member(s) leave project	2	8	Discuss succession and backup for key members with individual line-managers	G
I	Key sponsor or stakeholder leaves company	1	8	Discuss succession and backup for key staff with responsible directors & Board	G

Figure 2.10b Project risk summary

	Risk summary	Comments
1	Medium	If areas of concern addressed rapidly, will migrate to "low risk"
2	Sales organization will not adopt changes	Need to work with Sales Director on this one.
3	Most obvious solutions will have a high capital cost	Cannot really comment until we have a set of solutions
4	Project will not deliver adequate improvement	Need to verify expected performance improvement, also establish "voice of customer" input

Figure 2.11 Risk summary

hold a risk analysis session during each phase of DMAIC to check that they stayed on track and that the team could see a sustained reduction in risks through the project.

When should you perform risk analysis? Probably at least once in each phase of a DMAIC project. This means that risk assessment is not confined to the time when you are actually defining the change required, but also as you decide on the best solution and its implementation.

Team targets and training

The Define phase of a Six Sigma project is also the "forming" stage of a team. At the forming stage the project manager and sponsor are making decisions on resourcing. They have to decide skills, the number of people, and what their roles in the team will be. Typically the project manager will decide what team he wants and the project sponsor will help him or her to secure time for these people. The project manager needs to secure project budgets and people who can work full time and part time on the project. Having selected the right people, the project manager needs to build the team's commitment delivering the project and the required financial benefits.

The project team will usually meet first at a kick-off meeting. It is important that this meeting is well organized and that there is a clear agenda. Many a project manager has laid down the first signs of the success or failure of a project by the way in which they have handled the kick-off meeting.

Training is a crucial factor in the successful implementation of Six Sigma projects. It is critical to communicate both the "why" and the "how" of Six Sigma as early as possible, and provide the opportunity to people to improve their comfort level through training classes.

C. Hendricks and R. Kelbaugh, "Implementing Six Sigma at GE" (1998)

SMART VOICES

When the team comes together for the first time there will be fairly complex interactions between the people. Some may be tentative and unsure about exactly what there role is compared to everyone else. If some of the team have worked together before they will have preconceptions about each other, positive or negative. If they work well together, they could form a team within the team. This is a difficult stage and needs to be handled carefully if there is to be a smooth transition into an effective project team.

Make sure you allow enough time, at work and socially, for the team members to get to know each other. The Project Charter gives the team its focus, it is always good to involve team members in helping to develop it. It is important to make sure that meetings work to clear agenda and that time limits for activities such as brainstorming are set and adhered to. Dave set out the targets for his team – see Figure 2.12. It was important to him that all team members agreed to have their contribution judged against these targets.

Dave had now completed all the background activities in Define, agreed the Project Charter and he was now ready for the Define phase checklist.

	Overall team targets	Comments
1	Measurable improvement within 6 months	Manage via newly established metrics
2	All project deliverables achieved on-time and within budget	Manage via Project Plan and regular status reporting
3	Establish best practice and best metrics	Roll them out to USA and Asia Pacific
4	Ensure new level achieved is absolute minimum for future Delivery Performance	Manage via newly established metrics, work with QA
5	Obtain positive Customer Satisfaction input	Sales can lobby the "big 5" once we are into "Control" phase

Figure 2.12 Team targets and training

Define – the checklist

Teams bring each stage in the DMAIC process to a formal conclusion when they are able to answer the main questions raised in a checklist prepared for each phase. This ensures that the project sponsor is involved continuously and that the team progresses into the next stage with no significant loose ends. The Black Belt is responsible for ensuring that the team is aware of the requirements set out in the checklist and for ensuring that the project sponsor understands what is required from him/her. Many Black Belts have complained over the years about how difficult it can be to get sponsor access and time. This can be a problem, but it is best tackled by agreeing with the sponsor as early as possible in the project the best way to work together. The Black Belt and project

---

Why do projects have phases, gates and checklists?

All projects face significant challenges and even the best idea can be difficult to implement. Also, there will be learning during a project that may cause the project team, project manager or project sponsor to suggest a change in direction. Dividing projects into phases is a way to break a project into logical chunks with the flexibility to fine tune direction and project activities. Gates are required to check whether a project has delivered its objectives within a phase and to provide a formal checkpoint for management direction and decision-making. Gates also provide an opportunity to review investments levels and priorities. Checklist are useful for two reasons; firstly they take the guesswork out of what needs to be done to achieve objectives – all checklists must be declared early so that everyone involved knows what has to be achieved to proceed or to complete. Secondly, checklists are very good at making sure all the difficult questions are asked and answered honestly. Some of the biggest dangers faced by projects in delivering financial benefits are the difficult questions that no one asks and the honest answers that project teams are sometimes allowed to avoid!

SMART
ANSWERS
TO TOUGH
QUESTIONS

	Required outputs	Project managers comments	S	Sponsor comments	Y/N
1	*Project Charter.* Is the Project Charter complete and approved by the sponsor?	Charter complete, need to ensure there is no "mission creep" as project runs	G	Happy with this	Y
2	*Goal Statement.* Is the problem and the goal statement/objective clearly defined?	Objective defined, need to ensure we drive to specific goals – no blurring	G	OK with scope just now, need to ensure we stay in the achievable zone	Y
3	*SIPOC/Process Map:* Are the key customers, suppliers and processes clearly identified?	Yes, but SIPOC and process maps seem to do the same thing – duplicate	G	Read the text books, need to use both!!!	N
4	*Lessons learned.* Has the project team exploited existing knowledge from expert advice and similar projects?	Previous (unsuccessful) projects were reviewed during the Brainstorming	G	Management support assured, team working OK	Y
5	*Cost–benefit.* Is the project a priority and supported with a strong cost/benefit estimate?	Cost estimates OK, should review at the end of each phase to ensure we stay on track	G	Project has been justified over three years.	Y
6	*Resources:* Is the project adequately resourced with people, and is the project budget reasonable?	Team is good, budget looks OK, should review during "Improve" phase	G	Agree on re-review plans	Y
7	*Risk:* Have barriers to change, key risks and open issues been identified and acted upon?	Identified, still working with Sales Organization on "acceptance" of changes	A	Agree on re-review plans	N
8	*Team:* Are team and individual contribution targets and rewards clearly specified?	Not all contributions are specified, we have the key ones	G	Do we need them all formally completed?	Y

Figure 2.13 The Define checklist for Blue Computers

9	*Stakeholders*: Are key project stakeholders in support of the project proceeding?	Yes so far. Need senior Management to maintain drive and focus	G	Also need program manager to maintain drive and focus!	Y
10	*Plan*: Is the plan for Measure & Analyse robust and is the timescale feasible?	Looks good so far, all the appropriate tools have been considered	G	Agree, review during M&A phase activities	Y
11	*Concerns*: Are there any areas of outstanding concern?	Sales Organization acceptance; achievability of performance goal	A	Need to fix these!	N
	Conclusion	Date submitted	Date approved	Sponsor comments	S
	ONGOING VALIDITY - Is this still a valid project and should it proceed?	05-Feb-01	07-Feb-01	Go to next phase	G

Figure 2.13 *Continued*

team can also do a lot to make it easy for the project sponsor to fulfil their role.

Dave Spencer sat back and looked at the Define checklist (Figure 2.13). His project sponsor had just signed it off as complete. "One down, three more checklists to go!" he thought to himself. The team had worked well and had completed the phase in good time. The Measure & Analyse phases were going to be hard work but they had a good foundation. He had also found the electronic sign-off procedures had helped him to get fast decisions and advice from his project sponsor. This had meant that they had been able to conclude some of the easier project outputs quickly and to devote more of the team's time to the more difficult tasks.

By the end of the Define phase, Dave was pleased with the way the team

How do I use checklists to ensure a phase is completed?

- *Required outputs – States the major areas that must be addressed to enable the project to complete this phase and to begin the next phase?*

- *Project manager comments – What comments would the project manager include to support completion of this area on the project?*

- *Sponsor comments - Are there any comments that the sponsor would like to add?*

- *Y/N (Yes/No) – Has this deliverable been completed to the satisfaction of the sponsor?*

- *Conclusion – Dates of submission and approval by sponsor along with the sponsor's conclusion.*

was working. He and the project sponsor agreed that there were some areas of Six Sigma that the project sponsor did not have enough experience to sign-off as complete. They agreed to involve a Master Black Belt to review any complex statistical work in the next phases of the project.

So far so good, thought Dave as the team headed off for a few celebratory beers at the local pub. "When travelling down the fairway of life, take some time out to smell the roses" he had been told. Now seemed like a good time to be spending some social time with the team. There was still plenty to do but he now knew a bunch of people who could fix things. Measure & Analyse starts tomorrow!

Dave was also considering signing up for Master Black Belt (MBB) training after this project. He knew that the first few MBBs would get their pick of the best projects. He was excited by the idea of being able to contribute to multiple projects at one point in time.

3

DMAIC – The Measure & Analyse Phases

Data collection and analysis is the art and the science of Six Sigma. There are many best practice tools available to help project teams in the Measure & Analyse phases. These tools need good data. The team will analyse the root causes of problems and create a fact based foundation for developing solutions.

The Measure & Analyse phases are often split into two distinct phases in Six Sigma projects. We have put them together because of the interactive and iterative nature of Measure & Analyse. In many ways, these phases are about bringing facts and logic to areas that may be clouded in company history and accepted wisdom/myths. During these phases, answers to some specific questions will be structured and reported. It is also important to remember that the quality of outputs depends on the project members developing

SMART QUOTES

Those who have knowledge, don't predict. Those who predict, don't have knowledge.

Lao Tzu

into a team. At the outset of the measure phase the team is still likely to be at the "norming" stage of becoming a team. It is important that the team settles quickly into the tasks of measuring and analysing problems and solutions. Measure & Analyse is about getting into the details of facts and analysis as well as building an effective team that can convince others to accept their solutions.

During the Measure & Analyse phases the project team will produce a number of key outputs:

- Baseline performance data and key measures

- Operational data definitions

- Sigma level calculations

- Comparative best practices and benchmarks

- Detailed process maps

- Root cause analysis

- Analysis insights and conclusions

- Validated problem statement and solution options.

The project team will work on structuring and manipulating the key data that will be required for fact based analysis and conclusions. Supporting activities will include:

- Data collection planning and execution

- Sampling and Gage R&R (explained later in this chapter)

- Analysis tool selection and use

- Filing key analysis files for ease of future access

The team will use a variety of qualitative and quantitative analytical tools in the Measure & Analyse phases. Some of these tools can look pretty scary to people who are new to Six Sigma. However, don't worry! Remember that most of these tools have been around for a long time, there are lots of people who can help and there are good worked examples for many of them showing best practices in the appendix of this book. Also, there are people like Master Black Belts available who can help with the complex statistics. In our experience, most projects do not require complicated statistical analysis and when they do there are plenty of people who want to help you with the challenge.

Dave Spencer smiled as the last team member entered the room. It had been a good evening out and everyone was on time for the Measure & Analyse meeting. The team looked keen to get stuck into the next phase. Dave had also just been given the name of a Master Black Belt who would be available for the project on a part time basis. Dave suspected that there were a couple of areas of deep statistics where their skills would be needed.

Dave started the session by reminding the team about the problem they were trying to solve – how was Blue Computers going to improve on time delivery and customer satisfaction. Last week there had been more grim warnings from another customer of the likely consequences of continuing the status quo. Harry had been muttering darkly again about "something will have to change or something will have to change."

Data Requirements and Collection

Dave challenged the team to brainstorm the key questions that would need to be answered and the data that would be required to support the answers (see Figure 3.1). He was pleased with the speed that they came

	Key questions	Data requirements	Analysis methods	Y/N
1	What is the size of the issue	EMEA delivery metrics for the last 3 months	Metrics reporting package	Y
2	What are the key causes of the issue	Stated cause of error on reports	Pareto and histogram	Y
3	What parts of the organization own the problem(s)	Process detail	Process mapping/analysis. SIPOC analysis	Y
4	What do the current metrics tell us about the process	Internal process metrics/data	Brainstorming with data & SWOT	Y
5	What root causes are evident	All available data on trends etc.	Cause and effect ("fishbone")	Y
6	Are there any trends by product or customer or Country	Historical data sliced by Product, customer, Country	Pareto and histogram	Y
7	How does supply-chain performance impact Blue Computers' delivery performance?	Supplier performance metrics	Trend analysis by management	N

	Data requirements – slicing	Who	What	Where	When
1	EMEA delivery metrics for the last 3 months	Logistics and QA	Summaries	UK, France, Germany, Spain	Weekly for past 3 months
2	Stated cause of error on reports	Logistics and QA	Summaries	UK, France, Germany, Spain	Past 3 months
3	Process detail	Logistics and QA	Process steps	UK, France, Germany, Spain	N/A
4	Internal process metrics/data	Logistics, & QA	Summaries	UK, France, Germany, Spain	Past 3 months
5	All available data on trends etc.	Logistics and QA	Summaries	UK, France, Germany, Spain	Past 3 months
6	Historical data sliced by product, customer, Country	Sales, Order Fulfilment, QA	Summaries	UK, France, Germany, Spain	Past 3 months
7	Third-party supplier delivery performance	Supply Chain Management	Delivery vs. Commit	UK	Past 3 months

Figure 3.1 Key questions and data slicing

up with a result. They also ran through the required data slicing – the who, what, why and when of the data segments that they would need for the project.

It is important early in the Measure phase to get on top of the data collection challenge. There is a set of data collection issues that are common to most projects:

- Don't try to "boil the ocean" – you will not have the time to analyse everything, so use a set of key questions to focus attention and to reduce your data collection workload.

- Maximize the use of existing data – this is important because it is both available and already accepted in the company.

- Make friends with Finance – they will have to sign off your financial numbers at some stage, so use data that they will recognize. Finance is a good source of good data and people who can help your project.

- Look for external validation – external data particularly from customers or competitors always carries greater weight than internal data. Think through good sources of data and ways of getting hold of it.

- Try to automate new data collection as far as possible – look for ways to collect data from information systems or to get others to record data if possible.

Operational Data Definitions and Sampling

Once the data requirements are identified operational data definitions are required to explain clearly,

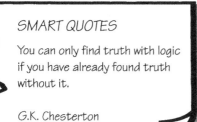

SMART QUOTES

You can only find truth with logic if you have already found truth without it.

G.K. Chesterton

and in more detail, what data is actually being collected and used. Many organizations suffer from the use of the same words to mean many different things – take for example the words process, operations and output. They can mean many different things and different parts of the company can have very different definitions. In our experience, project teams will save themselves a lot of time later in a project if they are clear in the measure phase about their data definitions.

Dave's team defined their key terms as shown in Figure 3.1

SMART VOICES

Data Definition

One project manager told us about a project that got its data definitions badly wrong . . .

A local authority decided to set up a central database of information about the land and property within its area. Each piece of land and property would have a unique number, a geographical identity and then links to all the information the authority held about it, from planning information to legal information and from its council tax information to the day on which it would have its rubbish removed.

The project team made good progress down a number of fronts until it became apparent that no one had yet agreed a precise definition of a unit of land or property. Was it a block of flats or each individual flat? In multiple occupations, indeed, was it a single room apartment? Just in time they stopped the project until they could agree a proper definition of terms.

	Operational data definitions	Detailed description	Verified
1	Actual delivery	Actual delivery of each product compared with the promised delivery, expressed as percentage on-time/early/late, of all shipments	Y
2	Supplier performance	Delivery performance from key suppliers compared with the contracted delivery, expressed as delivery metric	Y
3	Customer feedback	Sales will elicit direct customer feedback on selected deliveries – verbal/non-metric data	Y
4	Order Entry process performance	The ability to enter customer orders accurately and rapidly, to filter out "illegals" and to rapidly feed back on any issues	Y
5	Order commit process performance	The ability to provide the customer with accurate/achievable/specific delivery commitments based on accurate and timely input from Sales/Supplier/Manufacturing	Y
6	Merge-in-transit and Hub operations	The ability to get all the component parts of any given order into and out of the distribution hub and to the customer just-in-time and in line with the Commit	Y
7	Cash-to-cash cycle time	The ability to minimize the cycle time from cash out (payment) for raw materials to cash in (payment) for goods sold to customers	Y
8	Minimized inventory	The ability to operate with minimal inventory holding and cost liability, using Vendor Managed inventory and just-in-time processes	Y

Figure 3.1 Key terms for Blue Computers

Sampling

Sampling is the process of using a subset of data within an overall population to represent the larger population. It is important because it enables project teams to analyse and draw conclusions from data without having to collect detailed data on the entire population. Acceptable sample sizes can be calculated using statistical techniques (see the appendix for more details on sampling).

In moving towards sampling, the team should have a clear definition of what is being measured and first thoughts about how the data is going to be collected. Another part of the preparation of the team's sampling plan is slicing – the process of breaking data down into groups based on specific criteria. Criteria could include areas such as type of data (e.g. invoices, production reports, customer service complaints), time (e.g. day, week, month, quarter), location (e.g. plant, country, region) and owner (e.g. function, department, entity). Stratification is important in Six Sigma because it enables teams to create much greater visibility around what is going on in a process.

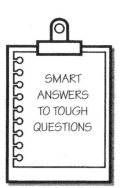

SMART
ANSWERS
TO TOUGH
QUESTIONS

What are the main sampling types?

Random sampling is the process of sampling where data points are selected totally at random. This approach to sampling is designed to reduce sampling bias. Sampling bias is the impact of factors that can cause a sample to be invalid. Bias is present in all samples; the objective is to sample in a way that keeps bias to a minimum. A sample that is not valid due to bias is described as a biased sample. It is important for project teams to design a sampling approach that minimizes bias.

Gage R&R to Validate Data

Gage R&R is a system used to validate the way that the measurement system is being used. It is a set of trials to assess the reproducibility and repeatability of the measurement system. As a general rule measurements should be precise, non-biased, repeatable, reproducible and stable. It is important because it helps to ensure that the data the team is using is the right data. Say, for instance, you ran a bottling plant and were having problems with leaking bottles. You need to know whether the problem is one of three things: bad closures, putting too much in the bottles or the bottles are being supplied too small. As part of the measures to establish the cause it is important that the people who are measuring the bottles for volume and other dimensions should be measuring the same things in the same way. Gage R&R will tell you whether they are or not. There is no point proceeding to the next stage of analysis until the measurement system is stable. (See appendices for more detail on Gage R&R calculations.)

Data Collection Plans and Files

It is important that the team should have a good data collection plan. The operational data definitions give a clear statement of what data needs to be collected, the plan covers the practical side of how it is actually collected. A good data collection plan aims to collect just the right amount, of the right data, covering the right data segments and timings, and to record it in electronic formats that are easy to access and manipulate. This is not as easy as we make it sound!

The basis of a good data collection plan is the right questions, right slicing and a good structure for storing the data. A good data collection plan will include:

- Key questions to answer

- What data

- Unit of measures

- Data type (e.g. quantitative or qualitative)

- Measurement method

- Timescale information

- Responsibilities

	Data requirements	Data collection worksheet	File location	Comment	Go
1	EMEA delivery metrics for the last 3 months	EMEA shipments Q3-00, Q4-00, Q1-01, Q2-01	Q/Shared/DelivFY01/ shipments.doc	Logistics Ops Metrics (UK)	
2	Stated cause of error on reports	Delivery/predictability Pareto	Q/Shared/SS/Blue02/ Pareto.doc		
3	Process detail	Delivery/predictability process points	P/Shared/Ger_Dist/ Proc_FY01.xls	Logistics & OM metrics (Germany)	
4	Internal process metrics/data	Logistics & Distribution internal controls summary	P/Shared/Ger_Dist/ Summ_Metric_FY01.xls	Logistics & OM metrics (Germany)	
5	All available data on trends etc	Quality Assurance analysis spreadsheets	Q/Shared/DelivFY01/ QAtrend.doc	6 Sigma team – QA metrics (EMEA)	
6	Historical data sliced by Product, customer, Country	Distribution closure reports	Q/Shared/DelivFY01/ sliced.doc	Logistics EMEA reporting (UK)	
7	Supplier performance metrics	Supplier metrics reports	Q/Shared/SCM/Metrics/ FY01/UK.doc	Supply Chain Management reporting system (UK)	

Figure 3.3 Data collection plan

- Sources

- Sample information

Once the data collection plan has been put into action, the team must have clear standards for where it is going to record and store the data. Dave's team was very much on top of this task. They had appointed a knowledge manager and all data was held within a single data repository for the project. Everyone on the team knew what was available, where it was and how to gain access to it (Figure 3.3). "This certainly makes delegation of analysis tasks a lot easier" thought Dave.

How do I calculate my level of sigma?

This calculation is relatively simple particularly if you can use Excel. First you have to calculate DPMO, defects percentage and process yield.

Defects per million opportunities (DPMO) = (total number of defects/total number of process opportunities) × 1,000,000.

Your defects percentage = (total number of defects/total number of process opportunities) × 100.

Your process yield = (100 − defects percentage)%.

Use Excel to calculate the sigma level using the following formula: σ = NORMSINV[1 − (total number of defects/total number of process opportunities)] + 1.5. The result will give you a sigma level assuming a shift of 1.5 for all values of z.

For example 230 defects per million is 5 sigma: 5.00 = NORMSINV[1 − (230/1,000,000)] + 1.5).

(NORMSINV in Excel returns the inverse of the standard normal cumulative distribution, the distribution has a mean of 0 and a standard deviation of 1).

SMART
ANSWERS
TO TOUGH
QUESTIONS

Calculating Current Sigma Levels and Process Capability

During the Measure & Analyse phases the project team should establish the current sigma levels for the key processes being analysed. This requires the team to be clear about units of data, number of opportunities and defect definitions. The sigma calculation can look complicated but in reality it is very simple if you use a software package like Microsoft Excel (see Smart Stats). Once the sigma levels have been calculated, the team should discuss or brainstorm the potential improvement opportunity. Many DMAIC projects struggle to move sigma levels beyond five sigma – these types of projects may require greater levels of innovation to achieve Six Sigma quality levels. We will discuss this later in the Design for Six Sigma chapter.

Week	1	2	3	4	5	6	7	8	9	10
OFE	126,000	126,000	126,000	126,000	126,000	126,000	126,000	126,000	126,000	126,000
DPMO	21,889	19,230	22,833	26,942	22,833	20,089	23,809	24,818	14,587	19,230
% "pass"	62	65	61	57	61	64	60	59	71	65
Sigma	3.5	3.57	3.49	3.47	3.49	3.55	3.48	3.47	3.68	3.57

Figure 3.4 Project sigma levels

Dave looked at the sigma calculations that the team had calculated for the last 10 weeks (Figure 3.4). "3.4–3.7 sigma isn't going to keep our customers as customers" he told the team. He remembered from his Black Belt course how Motorola had described the impact of four sigma on a number of processes (see Figure 3.5). We need a chart like this for our project he told the team. The important thing is to understand and document the implications.

The team should also look at process capability. This can be defined as being the level of variation in a process relative to the required specification. The specification is usually defined in terms of customer

	Process area	Current sigma level	S R	Implications
1	Lost letters	4	R	20,000 per hour
2	Incorrect surgical operations	4	R	5,000 per week
3	Bad landings at major airports	4	R	2 per day
4	No electricity supply	4	R	7 hours per month
5	Wrong prescriptions	4	R	200,000 per year

Figure 3.5 Motorola sigma examples

requirements. As a general rule the project team should analyse process capability to identify opportunities to improve average performance and to reduce variation around the average (e.g. better and tighter performance).

All companies can benefit from a review of their aims and strategies and of their associated methods, processes and level of success. Collaboration with an independent outsider who is not trapped by historical prejudices and knowledge of constraints can provide a fresh viewpoint. The problem is that the review has to be carried out by people armed not only with sound knowledge of measurement and analytical methods but also with the ability to communicate the importance of the project and of their findings.

G.J. Hahn, "The impact of Six Sigma improvement" (1999)

SMART VOICES

Baseline Performance Measures

Dave looked at some existing charts that analysed delivery performance

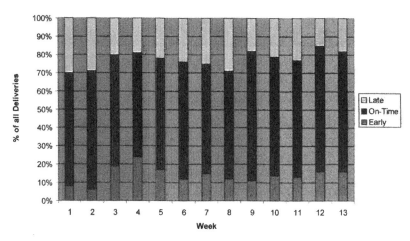

Figure 3.6 Delivery performance in one quarter

(Figure 3.6). Looks like some good baseline data – with plenty of scope for improvement, he thought.

 One of the key activities in the Measure phase is the documentation of baseline measures. Dave emphasized to the team the need to be clear about the measures, the current baseline and the source of the data (see

Baseline/process measures	Value	Source	S	Implications
1				
2				
3				
4				
5				

Figure 3.7 Baseline process measures

Figure 3.7). He told the team "If we can get this right at this stage, it will make our lives a great deal easier during the Improve phase."

Best Practices and Benchmarks – The Other Perspective

Best practices and benchmarks can be invaluable in helping project teams to establish the case for business change. Best practices tend to be descriptions of optimum ways to conduct processes (e.g. Dell's direct supply and build to order model for PCs is a best practice compared to traditional build to forecast models). Best practices can be either within a company or from an external company. Some best practices are difficult to measure but their use should be strongly encouraged and rewarded. Most companies would benefit significantly just from applying best practices, already in use in other parts of the company, more widely across the whole organization. Best practices are sometimes seen as lessons learned from one area of a business that could, and should, be applied more widely.

Benchmarking describes the processes and measures used to compare measured performance across companies and industries (e.g. Dell was able to achieve inventory turns of 56 compared to Compaq's 16). Benchmarks are very useful in showing differing levels of performance. However, they must be handled carefully to ensure that what is being compared is similar – otherwise benchmarking can be a blunt instrument. Benchmarks are almost always quantitative measures. There are many benchmarking companies that can provide comparative statistics. However, project teams need to understand the background to the measures to ensure that they are relevant.

Some words of warning on best practices and benchmarking. Teams may have difficulty in agreeing what best practice is and best practice will change over time. Benchmarking is also time consuming (unless someone else has done it for you) and teams need to be careful not to get caught out by "analysis paralysis". The best "rule of thumb" is to establish best practices and benchmarks quickly using existing data, reference visits and email requests. Focus on the major differences, the causes behind the variations and the implications this raises for the project.

Dave's team had found some interesting examples of comparative best practices and benchmarks – see Figure 3.8.

Why are statistics important?

Statistics is concerned with the collection, analysis, interpretation and presentation of data. Procedures in statistical quality engineering make use of actual data and objective mathematical principles so decisions arising from them are based on facts rather than, say, subjective feeling or opinions.

T.N. Goh, "An efficient empirical approach to process improvement" (1993)

Let the analysis begin

For Dave's team, the data collection activities were a time-consuming but necessary part of the DMAIC process. Analysing the data is going to be a lot more fun than collecting, thought Dave – hopefully! The first

What are the best practices	Source	I/E	Implications
1 100% on-time delivery	Industry standards	E	Can learn how Dell and Asda do it, to emulate their success
2 100% delivery predictability	Blue Computer US reports	I	Can adopt US practices where appropriate
3 Maximized inventory turns	Computer and food retail	E	Learn how Dell and the food industry do it, supplier management?
4 Minimized cash-to-cash cycle time	IT	E	Learn from Dell and other IT vendors (competitors)
5 Supplier/product merge at point of use	Automotive	E	Learn from Ford/GM/Nissan

What are the key benchmarks	Source	I/E	Implications
1 Food and consumables – distribution	Asda, M&S	E	Lessons can be learned
2 Direct computer – delivery model	Dell and Gateway	E	Ultimate industry benchmark/target for Blue Computers world wide
3 Automotive industry – inventory turns of 73 in assembly plants	Ford, GM, VW	E	Need to look at automotive techniques
4 Blue Computer US – distribution model	Blue Corporate.	I	First level target for Blue Computers in EMEA
5 Inventory Turns – Dell inventory turns of 56	Dell and various	E	Need to increase inventory turns

Figure 3.8

stage of analysis was a simple one, confirming which analytical tools to use where and why. Dave remembered the advice of the Master Black Belt: "Don't try and use every analysis tool that we have taught you –

	Basic qualitative tools	Where would you use it?	Why would you use it?
1	Fishbone diagram	To determine root causes and contributors	Takes project from symptom to root cause
2	SIPOC	To determine where in the organization to focus effort	Identify the key process steps
3	Detailed process map	To determine where in the organization to focus effort	Identify the process steps in need of corrective action or redesign
4	Issues/structure tree		
5	Kano analysis		
6	Forcefield analysis		
7	Day-in-the-life-of studies		
8	SWOT analysis	To determine what the current metrics tell us about the process	Relative strengths etc. of the process – using actual data
9	Decision analysis		
10	Moments of truth		

Figure 3.9

just focus on the ones you need to answer your key questions. You only need to do enough analysis to prove your points. Anything over that is unnecessary effort."

Dave scanned down the list that the team had prepared for him (Figure 3.9). He could see that they would be using fishbone and process mapping tools and then using bar charts and Pareto analysis to analyse the numerical data. He was pleased that the team was using tools that they were all comfortable with. We can save the more advanced tools for later in the analysis – he thought.

Most tools to support Six Sigma have generally been around for years, there are few specific Six Sigma tools – they are more of a collection of the best tools within one method. Analytical tools can be divided into five major categories:

- Basic qualitative tools – e.g. fishbone, process map

- Basic quantitative tools – e.g. histogram, ANOVA

- Advanced analytical tools – e.g. Design of Experiments (DoE) and QFD

- Project management tools – e.g. project plan templates and interview workbook

- Financial tools – business case templates and financial standards

The project team can save a great deal of time by using standard templates for these tools. They can be found in Microsoft Excel or MINITAB. In this book, we make use of many Excel templates that have been designed for Six Sigma projects by Continuous Innovation Culture (info@ci-c.com)

Basic Qualitative Analysis Tools

The Six Sigma toolbox is made up of a wide range of best practice tools that can be applied to most business problems. The basic qualitative tools are listed in the table above and worked examples of the main tools are in the appendix. Dave's team quickly expanded the simple process map that they had created in the Define phase (Figure 3.10). They used standard process mapping shapes and "swim lanes" to show the movement of activities between functions.

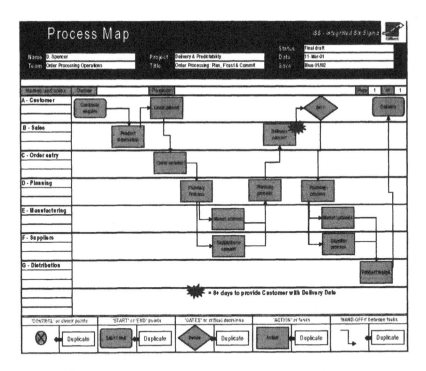

Figure 3.10 Process map

Why do we map processes?

Process mapping is a visual analytical tool designed to enable project teams to map and analyse processes at differing levels of detail. The process maps allows key steps to be mapped out to increase the project teams understanding of key flows and six key factors: inventory, costs, revenues, working capital, time and quality measures. Process mapping should also focus on areas such as the number of steps, number of physical handovers and the value of activities. Physical process flow charting is often referred to as a brown paper/post-it note exercise (from the roll of paper used to stick post-it notes to). Automated flowcharting can be created using packages such as Excel, PowerPoint and Visio. Project teams should be careful to focus attention on the right level of detail and critical process measures.

Dave was keen that the team should produce a root cause analysis using a fishbone diagram (Figure 3.11). It was the most useful qualitative tool that he had encountered on his Black Belt training. Somehow it seemed to pull everything together into a single simple format.

Dave checked to see that the team was drawing out implications and conclusions from their analysis. He remembered that a common problem on Six Sigma projects was that teams spend too much time analysing data and creating graphs and not enough time focusing on the implications of their conclusions (Figure 3.12). He checked through their suggested actions and thought about his approaching progress review with the project sponsor. "There will be lots to show at this next review" – he thought to himself.

The project team also worked through a SWOT analysis, looking at the strengths, weaknesses, opportunities and threats of Blue Computer's current position (Figure 3.13). The team concluded that the key motivator for customers was predictability of delivery not speed. They also

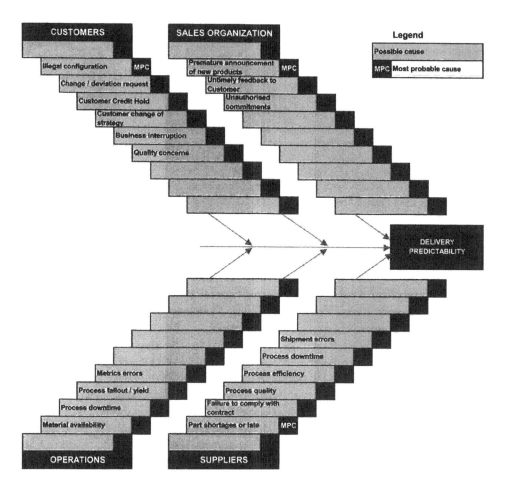

Figure 3.11 Fishbone diagram

noted that competitors were improving their delivery predictability and that Blue Computers had to respond.

When and why would you use a Fishbone or Ishikawa diagram

A cause-and-effect diagram is a visual analytical tool (sometimes called a fishbone or Ishikawa diagram) that displays the grouped causes (fishbones) that contribute to a problem (the head of the fish). It is a very useful for illustrating the combination of factors that contribute to a problem. Most Six Sigma projects will require the project team to produce a root cause analysis. It is important to identify main causes or MPC – most probable causes. There are standard tools available to map fishbone diagrams these can save project teams time.

SMART
ANSWERS
TO TOUGH
QUESTIONS

Priority	Contributor to Poor Delivery Performance	Potential root causes	Agreed Priority Root Cause(s)	Action Plan	Owner
1	Sales re-schedule	Customer re-schedule			
		Unachievable commit			
		Credit hold			
		Export hold			
			Unachievable commit	Train Sales team in use and operating parameters of the Forecast and Commit # Processes	Sales & Logistics & HR
2	Supplier de-commit	Material shortage			
		Transportation issue			
		Planning & forecasting issue			
		Process yield			
		Engineering changes			
		Credit hold			
		Export hold			
			Planning & forecasting issue	Conduct review with all key Suppliers to emphasise: a) VMI & JIT requirements; b) Contractual obligations; c) Supplier Metrics & # the enforcement of Performance	Supply-Chain Management
3	New Product not available	Release delays			
		Pre-release announcements			
			Pre-release announcements	Train Sales team in use and operating parameters of the New Product Introduction # Process	Sales & Engineering & NPI
4	Processing Error	Input error			
		Operator fault			
		Corrupt data			
			Operator fault	Review Order Processing processes and evaluate opportunities for training and re- # assignment	Logistics & HR

Figure 3.12 Root cause analysis

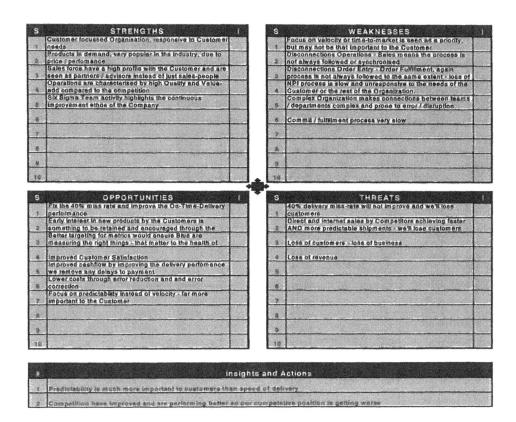

Figure 3.13 SWOT analysis

Basic Quantitative Analysis Tools

Six Sigma is well known for its focus on the use of statistical tools for project analysis. The statistical tools draw heavily on industrial statistics but most are easy to grasp with a little training or a background in basic statistics. We have put a number of explanations and worked examples of tools in the appendix to avoid breaking the flow of the Blue Computers case study. The main tools are listed in Table 3.1

The good news about quantitative tools is that there are great statistical analysis packages available that can do most of the hard grind of statistics for you. Indeed, it could be argued that most project team members need to know very little about setting up statistical analysis, but they do need to know how to interpret results and to draw out statistically sig-

Table 3.1 Basic quantitative tools

Basic quantitative tools	Where would you use it?	Why would you use it?
Control/run chart	Ongoing shipment operations as part of the standard metrics package	To monitor delivery performance and predictability, to take immediate action if any control limit is breached
Histogram	To narrow down the key causes	Obtain the relative impact of each cause
Pareto	To prioritize the cause	Obtain a relative priority for causes to be addressed
Scatter diagram		
Regression/correlation		
Probability distribution		
T-test		
Multivariate		
Chi square		
ANOVA		

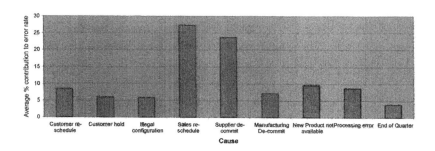

Figure 3.14 *Histogram of causes of delivery misses*

nificant conclusions. For instance, you rarely need to calculate R^2 squared in regression analysis these days. What you do need to know is how to tell if an R^2 score of 0.7 is significant (it is!).

Dave asked the team to show how the quantitative project data supported their root cause analysis conclusions. The team had put together some good examples of histograms analysing delivery misses (Figure

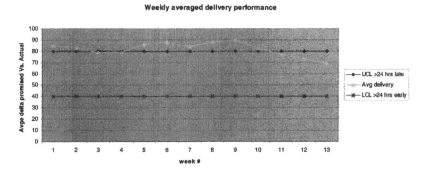

Figure 3.15 *Delivery performance*

3.14). Illegal configuration did not appear to be the major problem that had been suggested by the manufacturing managers at the beginning of the project.

The analysis of causes of delivery failure also showed a range of causes but a few that stood out as areas to be addressed.

The team looked at delivery performance over time using control charts (Figure 3.15). There were some clear problems that needed to be addressed.

Advanced Analytical Tools

Advanced statistical tools are required where there are complex interre-

What is Design of Experiment (DOE)?

DOE is a structured approach to understanding the impact of input factors (Xs) on the output (Y) of a process. Put simply – the aim is to vary the inputs in a systematic way to identify the key input factors that determine the output of a process. It is a way of evaluating the value of a factor or group of factors by controlling the process environment.

"To change a process for better performance, it is necessary to understand the input–output relationship. Input refers to parameters such as time, temperature and pressure that can be manipulated, and output refers to some quality indicator such as yield. Since most industrial processes are too complex to be analysed from first principles of science or engineering, very often experimental techniques must be used to obtain the needed relationship. A collection of statistical techniques known as design of experiments can be used to chart the best course of action to obtain the needed input–output relationship for process improvement."

S. Bisgard, "Industrial use of statistically designed experiments" (1992)

SMART
ANSWERS
TO TOUGH
QUESTIONS

lationships in the data. In these cases, advanced statistical analysis and other techniques can be used to analyse areas such as causality and correlation between variables. Most of the advanced techniques tend to be the preserve of experienced Black Belts and Master Black Belts. We have included examples for Design of Experiments and Quality Function Deployment in the appendices. These tools can be highly effective and should be used where required. They are generally less frightening to use than most people expect – what is generally required is careful management of the analysis process.

Analysis Tool Selection Matrix

We have put together an analysis tool selection matrix (Figure 3.16) to help you to select the right tools, for the right purpose and at the right phase of a project.

Experience has shown that teamwork and the right measurement selection are keys to good decision-making in projects. But equally important

What are the major tools used on projects?

Project tools can be divided into five main categories: basic quantitative analysis tools, basic qualitative analysis tools, advanced analysis tools, project management and financial tools. As a team member or project manager gains experience, their usage and familiarity with tools will change. The objective is that Green Belts and Black Belts will, over time, gain experience and confidence in using a variety of tools and techniques. At the end of the day, the important thing is that the right tools are used on the right projects. It is also important that the company is constantly growing the skills and knowledge of its pool of project managers and team members.

6 Sigma Tools Selector	Type	D	M	A	I	C	Other
Fishbone	Qual			x			
SIPOC	Qual	x					
Process Map	Qual	x		x			
Issues Tree	Qual			x	x	x	
CTQ Tree	Qual	x					DFSS
Kano	Qual	x		x			DFSS
Forcefield	Qual			x			
Day in the Life	Qual			x	x	x	
Moments of truth	Qual	x		x			
SWOT	Qual	x		x			
Decision Analysis	Qual			x	x		
Affinity	Qual	x		x	x		
Brainstorming	Qual	x		x	x		
Customer Survey	Qual	x					DFSS
Value Added Analysis	Qual			x			
Poke Yoke (mistake proofing)	Qual				x	x	
Process Sigma	Quant		x	x			
Process Capability	Quant		x	x			
GAGE R&R	Quant		x				
Control Chart	Quant		x	x	x	x	
Run Chart	Quant		x	x	x	x	
Process Control Charts	Quant					x	
Histogram	Quant		x	x	x	x	
Pareto	Quant		x	x	x		
Scatter	Quant			x			
Regression	Quant			x			
Probability Distribution	Quant		x	x	x	x	
T test	Quant			x			
Multivariate analysis	Quant			x			
Chi Square	Quant			x			
Hypothesis testing	Quant			x			
Yield analysis	Quant	x		x			
Input/Output matrix	Quant		x		x		
ANOVA	Quant			x			
Design of Experiments	Adv			x	x		
FMEA	Adv		x	x	x		
QFD	Adv	x		x			DFSS
Data Collection Plan	Project		x	x	x	x	
Data Collection Forms	Project		x	x	x	x	
Interview workbook	Project	x	x	x	x	x	
Stakeholder Analysis	Project	x					
Risk Summary	Project	x	x	x	x	x	
Solution Filter	Project				x		
Impact / Effort Filter	Project	x			x		
Project Plan	Project	x	x	x	x	x	
Change Plans	Project				x	x	
Communications Plan	Project	x			x	x	
Project Scorecard	Fin/Proj	x	x	x	x	x	
Business case	Fin				x	x	
Cost benefit analysis	Fin	x	x	x			
Benefits Segmentation	Fin	x	x	x	x	x	

Figure 3.16 Analysis tool selection matrix

is the need for clever and easy-to-understand displays of the data gathered and analysed. Too many times opportunities are lost or lessons not passed on to other individuals in the organization because of the poor display and communications of work done. It does not always come easily to project and scientific thinkers to communicate well, but being able to do so can often mean the difference between success and ineffectiveness. Teams should make their choice of tools in the light of this.

Drawing Out the Analysis Conclusions

The team was now ready to provide their answers to the key questions (Figure 3.17). They are able through the analysis to answer each of the questions and to provide sufficient evidence to support their conclusions. The conclusions are, of course, based around the key questions asked much earlier in the process. It is at this stage that detailed targets can be set for the improvement of the process. The process of drawing out conclusions is often hard work but it is critical to the future success of the project. The key is to keep asking the question – "So what?"

The project team then had to summarize the problems and root causes so that they could identify logical improvement opportunities. The root cause analysis has discovered a number of problems with the behaviour of the sales force rather than the physical hardware and software supply (Figure 3.18). These are areas that will need to be addressed in the next phase.

Finally the project team summarized its initial views on opportunity areas and potential targets for improvement (Figure 3.19). They are now in a position to define the improvement using a combination of the baseline performance measures and "to be" targets that look reasonable

Key questions	Answers	Supporting evidence
What is the size of the issue	60% of shipments on-time, 12% early, 28% late	Overall performance measures
What are the key causes of the issue	Reschedules & unrealistic commits by Sales; third party and manufacturing ops de-commits, order processing quality	Overall performance measures
What parts of the organization own the problem(s)	Sales organization, manufacturing operations, order fulfilment operations, supply management operations	Root causes found in all major parts of the organization
What do the current metrics tell us about the process	There are process disconnects	Numerous instances of orders failing to complete the OF/OM cycle; erroneous orders can get through
What root causes are evident	Sales are not complying with the commit process. Suppliers are not adhering to VMI & JIT contractual obligations	Key findings from team review of all data
Are there any trends by product or customer or country	No discernible trends, flat rate failure across all products/regions/customers	Nothing coming from the data

Figure 3.17 Answers to key questions

given benchmarking comparisons and the analysis of current performance.

Dave was pleased with what the team had produced. "Things have really come together" he said. He felt confident that the team's work would stand up well to the Measure & Analyse phases gate review that was going to take place over the next few days.

	Problems	Root cause	Required action
1	Orders delivered later/earlier than expected	Sales force making delivery commits prior to the completion of the planning process	Retrain sales ops, apply new performance metrics
2	Orders delivered later/earlier than expected	Sales force not adequately communicating with customer on new product availability or illegal configurations	Retrain sales ops, apply new performance metrics.
3	Orders not getting through the process cleanly	Order fulfilment process has gaps and overlaps	Map and re-engineer order fulfilment process
4	Third parties decommitting on promises	Third-party suppliers not complying with contractual obligations on vendor-managed inventory (VMI) or JIT	Review contracts and rules of engagement with key suppliers
5	Higher than expected proportion of "early" deliveries	Majority of early deliveries result from customer requested pull-ins	Stop counting these as defects in the performance reporting system

Figure 3.18 *Root cause summary*

Measure & Analyse Checklist

The time had come for Dave to get formal sign off for the Measure & Analyse checklist from the project sponsor. However, before the sponsor was going to sign-off the completion of the phase, Dave had to get two other approvals signed off. The Finance representative had already agreed to the baseline financial numbers in the project. The next person to talk to was the Master Black Belt (MBB).

Dave's meeting with the MBB went well. He took the MBB through the

Opportunity areas	Baseline (as is)	Target (to be)
Improve delivery performance	60% OTD, 12% early, 28% late	Minimum 95% OTD.
Ensure sales only commit a delivery when the commit or NPI/announce process has been completed	Sales team tend to announce and sell new products to customers before product release	Sales team only offer achievable commit dates
Fix the order fulfilment process, reduce cycle times and errors	Process suffers delays and is error prone	Process is 100% value add and error free
Review and upgrade supplier performance and adherence to contract	Supplier compliance patchy and re-active	Supply-base 100% compliant, proactively working to breakthrough
Remove spurious inputs from delivery performance metrics	Includes several inappropriate measures	Includes only relevant data, reviewed bi-annually for ongoing relevance

Figure 3.19 *Opportunity areas, baselines and targets*

project team's work and discussed their conclusions. The project sponsor had asked the MBB to check out the more complex statistics and data validity and the team had passed with "flying colours". The MBB agreed to sign off all the major outputs.

- Data collection requirements

- Data collection templates and files

- Analysis files (see appendix for analytical tools)

- Detailed process maps

- Best practices and benchmarks

- Root cause analysis

- Potential solutions options

The checklist is designed to ensure that the project sponsor is involved continuously and that the team continues into the next stage with no significant loose ends. The project sponsor questioned some of Dave's data because he had hoped that there would be more. Dave had to explain the gaps in the data and to show how the team had made great efforts to secure the best data available.

At the end of the Measure & Analyse phases, the project team will have a clear understanding of the problems with current processes and they will have concrete evidence to support the development of new process solutions. The team will now be ready to move into the Improve phase where it will develop its preferred solutions.

Dave smiled, that first beer at the pub was going to taste very good. The team was waiting for Dave to complete the project documentation and they had all agreed to go out for a project team meal that evening. The evening was bound to be entertaining – the team had been storing up project mistakes, quotes and jokes all month. The "project awards" were going to be fun. It was time for the team to blow off some steam. Then again, the Improve phase begins tomorrow. Being a Black Belt was a lot more interesting and fun than Dave had anticipated.

He had just heard from the training department that there was a space on the Master Black Belt course in two months' time. "This should be worth an extra bonus this year" he thought to himself "It will be hard work but, at least, you can see the rewards. There aren't many others who have managed to combine the training and project delivery so quickly."

	Deliverables	Project manager comments	S	Sponsor comments	Y/N
1	*Key questions and measures* – Has the team identified the key questions and what to measure?	Yes, there are seven major questions alluding to this project	G	Agree	Y
2	*Data definitions* – Are operational data definitions and samples clear and relevant? Have they been agreed with others?	Some data vague and anecdotal	A	Need to go with what we have	Y
3	*Data collection plan* – Has the team conducted a complete, effective and efficient data collection plan?	Will collect through existing metrics plus anecdotal input from Sales & customers	G	Not happy with "anecdotal" element, is there anything more empirical available?	Y
4	*Data collection worksheets* – Are the data collection worksheets well designed and are people capable of completing them? Is the sampling plan valid?	Use metrics package and analysis processes	G	What will be different from status quo?	Y
5	*Execution* – Is the execution of the data collection plan consistent and reliable?	As reliable data already exists this should be straightforward	G	Agree	Y
6	*Baselines and targets* – Have baseline measures been established and agreed?	Targets linked to goal of 95% on-time-delivery (OTD) and to cash-to-cash (C2C) cycle time of 42 days	G	Agree	Y
7	*Analysis* – Has the project team effectively analysed areas for improvement?	Extensive analysis with multiple tools	G	Agree, good job	Y
8	*Conclusions* – Are there clear quantitative measures available to support their conclusions?	Not in all cases, but confident enough to move forward	G	Agree	Y

Figure 3.20 Measure & Analyse checklist

9	*Root cause* – Is the root-cause analysis clear, prioritized and supported by clear evidence?	Analysis points clearly to five major root causes, some surprise as to the no. 1 issue		Agree but don't lose 2, 3 and 4 in pursuit of no. 1	Y
10	*Updated project plan* – Is the plan for Improve robust?	Project plan has slipped over last two phases, improve phase is good but need to accelerate process if we are to catch up		Yes, get the team to pick up the pace	Y
11	*Concerns* – Are there any areas of outstanding concern?	Sales team commitment a concern	A	Work with EMEA Sales Director	Y
Finance approval		**Date submitted**	**Fin**	**Finance comments**	**S**
Finance support – Does Finance agree that the financial data being used is valid?		19-Feb-01		Project data is valid and consistent with Finance numbers.	
Conclusion		**Date submitted**	**S**	**Sponsor comments**	**S**
Ongoing validity – Is this still a valid project and should it proceed?		25-Feb-01		Rationale remains strong in spite of limited shortcomings, should forge ahead.	

4

The DMAIC Process – Improve

The project team now moves forward into designing new solutions to address identified problems. They agree on their preferred options, set up a pilot and think through how to persuade others to implement the required changes

"Don't give me problems, just solutions!" is a good way to sum up the intent of the Improve phase. The project team has had the luxury of being an external observer of business problems. Now, they have to start taking responsibility for solutions. The Improve phase should be a lot of fun for the project team as well as being hard work. The phase is about prioritizing and testing solutions and building the case for change.

The Improve phase sets out to achieve four major things:

• Generate and test solution options

• Select preferred solutions

Why do we need to present options rather than a preferred solution?

Despite the lack of choice that Henry Ford famously made available to his customers – "You can have any color you want as long as it is black" – he trained his people in the opposite way, and insisted that any decision that anyone was going to ask him to make had to have alternatives.

- Build the case for change
- Build support for the required changes.

The Improve phase is about making decisions as a team. It may be that the team includes members who are naturally better decision-makers than others. In our experience, some people are confident enough to make a decision while others prefer to have them made for them. Whichever approach you favour, a standard decision making process can help the team to be more effective. Our suggested approach to decision making in Six Sigma is based on team decision making.

During the Improve phase the project team will produce a number of key outputs:

- Brainstormed solution options
- Solution filter
- Solution definition and business case
- Pilot plan and learnings
- Updated solution risk summary
- Improve checklist

We will look at each of these in turn.

Solution Options and the Solution Filter

Dave knew that the time had come to make some important decisions about which solutions the project team should design and implement to meet their objectives? He was confident that he had a team that was more than up to this task. "Time for a really good brainstorming session" thought Dave.

Teams sometimes find it hard to find options. Some people follow their gut instincts and more or less pre-empt the decision making process. The danger here is that they define one option in a way that is obviously a more likely solution than any other. Six Sigma calls for a rigorous approach to identifying and testing different solution options. It is important to use option development techniques that prevent any single individual dominating or constraining the range of options considered. Brainstorming techniques such as affinity diagrams and decision analysis can help to keep the "hopper" of options full.

Dave's team identified nine solution options for further evaluation. Some members of the team were clearly in favour of one or two of the ideas but there were others who were not convinced that these were the best solutions. Dave knew that it would be important to get all of the team to own the preferred solution. He had been given a two-stage solution filter framework by the Master Black Belt (Figure 4.1). The MBB favoured a first level evaluation approach based on VSAFE criteria (see below).

The team then ran this through the first level filter – using the VSAFE criteria for assessing the strength of each potential solution:

- *V for Value* – Looks at the expected impact on the bottom line. Will

	Top ten ideas	Description and impact on the project	V	S	A	F	E	%	R
1	Retrain the sales team	Ensure the sales team only commits delivery to the customer when the rest of the organization has agreed	8	6	8	6	7	70	A
2	Give Sales access to Oracle	Sales team would be able to see future availability and outlook on current deliveries	4	4	4	2	3	34	No
3	Give Sales a sign-off on NPI release	Sales team would be better informed on availability of new prods	5	7	8	3	4	54	No
4	Ensure all parties sign off on customer-commits	Operations would be able to agree delivery commits *before* the customer expectation is set	3	3	4	6	4	40	No
5	Amalgamate the OE and order fulfilment function	Current process gaps and interrupts would be eliminated (large separate project?)	7	6	3	3	6	50	No
6	Retrain the OE and OF functional staff	Current process gaps and interrupts would be minimized	5	6	8	6	7	64	B
7	Enforce VMI & JIT with supply-base	Suppliers would follow their own rules more strictly, availability and decommits would be minimized	5	6	5	7	6	58	?
8	Enforce supplier metrics	Feedback on poor performance to suppliers would have the weight of disqualification behind it	6	6	5	8	6	62	C
9	Revise delivery "failure" criteria	Ensure that only those failures that have a genuine customer impact and are also a direct result of Blue Computer errors are recorded and responded to	3	7	6	5	7	56	?

Figure 4.1 Solution options and filter

the solution deliver clear financial benefits in excess of implementation costs?

- *S for Suitable* – Examines how this idea contributes to the company's business strategy and business imperatives. Does the proposed solution fit with our business imperatives?

- *A for Acceptable* – The team should take a little time to think about how acceptable the stakeholders will find the idea. Will stakeholders agree with this solution option?

- *F for Feasible* – Checks that the idea is feasible given time and other constraints. Is it feasible to implement this solution in our organization?

- *E for Enduring* – The team needs to check the likely endurance of the proposed solution. Is the proposed solution option likely to be sustainable?

Each factor was scored out of 10 and then an average score calculated. From the VSAFE score the "top three" ideas were ranked as:

(A) Retrain the sales team in new processes

(B) Retrain the order entry and order fulfilment staff

(C) Enforce supplier metrics

The other solution options were graded as either GO or NO-GO depending on whether they were seen as worth recording by the team.

Dave now got the team to work through the second-stage filter. They developed a set of eight criteria for judging the value of the options and then brainstormed the weights for each selection criteria (Figure 4.2). Dave had been helped by advice from the MBB about good selection criteria and how the weights had been allocated in previous projects. When the team was satisfied with the criteria and weights they assess

	Weighted selection criteria	W	A	B	C	W×A	W×B	W×C
1	Cost	5	5	5	5	25	25	25
2	Timescale	8	5	3	3	40	24	24
3	Direct impact on delivery performance and predictability	10	4	4	4	40	40	40
4	Enhanced customer satisfaction	8	5	4	3	40	32	24
5	Improved cashflow	4	2	2	3	8	8	12
6	Reduction in OE/OF process cycle time	4	1	5	1	4	20	4
7	Reduction in OE/OF process defects	5	4	5	2	20	25	10
8	Alignment with corporate processes in EMEA	2	3	3	3	6	6	6
Weighted totals						183	180	145

Figure 4.2 Second-stage filter

each solution option. The result was very close between option A and option B. However, the most important thing was that the team agreed with the conclusion – some may not have had option A as their preferred option but they were now happy to support it as the team solution.

Pilot

By incorporating a pilot phase into the plan, a team will have a far less stressful and less error-prone time when it comes to rolling out the entire project. The pilot phase will have armed the team with the ammunition to demonstrate that the project is achieving the improvements it is seeking. It is important to choose the people for the pilot carefully, including sceptics as well as believers, if the pilot is to give the team an accurate indication of possible problems and objections. The people in a pilot can be a team's greatest ambassadors and agents for change if they are well treated and, perhaps, rewarded for their work in the pilot. The

SMART
ANSWERS
TO TOUGH
QUESTIONS

What do we need to know before we start a pilot project?

- What is the planned date that the pilot will start and how long will it run for?

- What will the impact be on the normal operation of the business?

Consider what time is needed for training of participants and what disruption the pilot could cause while people get used to the new process.

- Whose approval is needed before the pilot can be carried out?

These are normally the managers of all areas that will be involved or impacted by the pilot.

- What are the implications for the solution of this finding?

Consider if it the solution should be modified or if it makes the solution no longer the best one to take forward.

- What are the main phases of the pilot?

These should include documentation of the new process, training of the pilot team, the actual pilot run and review of the results.

- What is the key deliverable for this phase?

This can range from documentation to a fully trained team and from pilot results to improvement suggestions.

- What are the key areas of the process that the pilot gave important information on?

- What was the result of the pilot for this area?

- What are the implications for the solution of this finding?

team should not forget that the people on the pilot take some risks and will have gone to some trouble to be the guinea pigs.

Dave had not conducted a pilot in Blue Computers before so he decided to re-read the training manual. It reminded him of the key elements required. The definition of the pilot phase identifies the groups and individuals who will be involved, and the associated timing. In most instances, those involved in a pilot are pulled away from their normal functions. The project team must therefore estimate, with as much accuracy as possible, the impact of these absences on operations. It is also important that people involved in the pilot be able to see the rewards of taking part and not just the prospect of hard work.

Dave's team set out the plan that would underpin a successful pilot of the new processes. They quickly recognized that this was a significant piece of work. If they didn't get the pilot right, then there was a good chance their solution would be discarded – not because it was wrong but because the pilot failed to show its value properly. Dave had been helped by his project sponsor to get a good sales region for piloting the new processes. John Kelly was very good friends with the Regional Sales Manager and he promised to put good people onto the pilot and to be proactive in showing his support for the pilot. Dave was pleased at the level of top cover he was now getting from John. Like all good project sponsors, John had a knack for knowing when he could and couldn't add value to the project. The pilot definition and plan had been useful in helping John to talk the Regional Sales Manager through the pilot.

Dave had the team create a separate area in the project plan for the pilot. "We don't need a separate project plan, just an area in the plan that is devoted to the pilot" he told the team member responsible for maintaining the overall project plan.

A successful pilot gives the project team an important boost to their con-

Pilot definition		Comments	
Groups involved	Sales, Logistics, HR/Training		
Timing	Training in one EMEA Sales office at Q3 end (Apr-01)		
Operational impact	Training after quarter end to minimize impact on sales targets, training during weeks 1 and 2 of quarter ideal		
Required approvals	EMEA Sales Director, Sales Operations Line Managers and Logistics Director	Approval required no later than 15 Mar-01	

Pilot phases		Key deliverable	Comments	S
1	Confirm commit and forecasting processes	Current (revised) process defined and documented	Consider revision of OF process	
2	Plan training content	Complete training materials and worked examples for illustration	None	
3	Plan training schedule	Schedule for training all sales operators in UK	None	
4	Deliver training	All UK sales operators trained in current/revised commit processes	None	
5	Follow-up sessions	Feedback from trained sales operators on effectiveness of process	Review if feedback negative	

Figure 4.3 Pilot definition and deliverables

	Key areas	Result	Implications
1	Unrealistic commits	Stop trying so hard to please the customer at this stage, will be happier with accurate rather then rapid delivery	Have to reset expectations of what customer satisfaction really is
2	Premature announcement	Stop advising on new products before general availability is announced.	Sales should have an involvement in the NPI process
3	Operations let the customer down	Decommits caused by Operations or suppliers need to be more rapidly conveyed to Sales	Sales need to be more thoroughly in the loop
4	Operations let the customer down	Operations need to drive internal and supplier issues with maximum priority	Raise the profile of decommits to top priority

Figure 4.3 *Pilot definition and deliverables – continued*

fidence. They are now aware that the process can be implemented and that the results that flow from it are beneficial to the business. In addition, the data derived from the pilot can be used to prepare a pretty accurate business case for rolling the process out to business.

Dave was not surprised when the pilot proved to be a great success. "It's amazing how the combination of the right new processes, motivated people and the right top cover can make an impact so fast" he told the team. "We couldn't have planned this one better."

Solution Definition and Business Case

Following the pilot, it is now time for the team to conclude and document the new process designs and the business case for the solution. The solution definition should be concise and easy to understand (particularly for people who have not yet been involved in the project). The team should be very clear about what is to be done differently and the critical success factors for effective implementation of the new solution. The revised business case carries much more weight than the previous estimates as it now reflects the learnings from the real-life pilot study. The learnings also enable the team to document key assumptions and any limitations of the project. This will set the expectations for the team and the key stakeholders about the likely business case for the project. The business case is a vital document. It will have the single greatest impact on the likelihood of success in the implementation phase of the project. If it is strong, believable and acceptable, then the project team will have strong support for implementation.

Dave and the team had worked hard to produce a concise definition of the solution (Figure 4.4). They were clear about what needed to be done differently and they also knew that it was going to be challenging getting the Sales Director to accept a new commit process.

Dave knew how important the business case was going to be to the success of the project. He had included Melanie Rock, a member of Finance, in his team and she was now very much coming into her own. She had good relationships with other people in the finance department and she knew Tom Caswell well. Tom had been appointed as the Finance representative who would sign-off acceptance of the financial and business case numbers for the project. He was known for being a real stickler for detail and Melanie was pleased that he was satisfied with the team's numbers. He would be required to sign-off for Finance at the end of Measure & Analyse, Improve and Control.

Melanie was using a standard business case template that had been supplied by the Six Sigma team. It contained basic frameworks and details

Overall solution definition		
Retrain the sale force across EMEA in the new delivery commit process		
Key process elements	'What is to be done differently'	Critical success factors
1 Customer delivery commits	Sales team to ensure commit process is complete before informing customer	All commits to be realistic/achievable
2 New product availability	Sales team to verify new product availability using system before offering it to the customer	Operations need to drive internal and supplier issues with maximum priority
3 Schedule changes by Operations	Operations to ensure Sales agree schedule changes before accepting them	Operations schedule changes agreed by Sales and accepted by the customer
4 Schedule changes by third-party suppliers	Operations to ensure Sales agree schedule changes before accepting them	Operations schedule changes agreed by Sales & accepted by the customer
5 Supplier metrics	Supplier metrics to reflect performance and used to drive improvements	Suppliers adhere to VMI and JIT commitments so that availability is no longer an issue
6		
Key assumptions and project limitations		Reasons and comments
1 Sales teams across EMEA will all respond equally well to training		Cannot afford to have some teams ignoring the process, must be consistent
2 Application of the supplier metrics will have the desired impact on their performance		Suppliers need to reset their performance against Blue's requirements
3 In depth review of the OE/OF process still recommended though not directly achieved through this project		Too big for the scope of this project, but vitally needed
4		

Figure 4.4 Solution definition

on company standards such as hurdle rates, payback requirements and expected internal rates of return (IRR). Melanie knew that she would save a lot of time using the standard approach because it was a recognized best practice and all the key people in Finance knew how to use it. She had been pleased when Dave Spencer had given her time on the project to train the other team members on how to use the tool. She knew that it was important for all the team to understand the business case – "There is no point having one or two people who own the business case" she told Dave "It is a team business case and we must all be able to support it." She had just updated the business case summary in the project reporting tool (Figure 4.5).

3 year cost–benefit	Quarter 1	Quarter 2	Quarter 3	Quarter 4	Year 1	Year 2	Year 3
Capital costs	£261,500	£113,500			£375,000		
Operating costs		£63,332	£99,996	£99,996	£263,324	£399,984	£399,984
Operating benefits	£0	£111,500	£199,500	£199,500	£510,500	£798,000	£798,000
TOTAL	–£261,500	£65,332	£99,504	£99,504	£127,824	£398,016	£398,016
Company hurdle rate	8						
Project risk adjusted hurdle rate	7						
Payback period	12 months						

Figure 4.5 Project business case summary

Expected customer impact/intangible benefits
95% + customer deliveries arrive when promised
5% of early or late deliveries are fully known & understood by the customer, Sales and Operations
Management of supplier performance becomes simpler and more linear
Internal cash-to-cash cycle is enhanced

Figure 4.6 Intangible benefits summary

The business case showed a one-year payback. This was not going to be a difficult sell. The expected customer impact was very strong (Figure 4.6) and there were good targets for improved delivery performance.

Dave knew that some members of senior management would be interested in the customer impact benefits. However, he also knew that there were some people in Finance who would attach no value at all to these

SMART VOICES

Think of the impact on each stakeholder that each solution or idea implies. If many people will be impacted by the idea, is the team going to be able to contact all of them in a way that makes sense? Perhaps the team needs to decide at this stage how it is going to consult them. Will it take face to face meetings? Is there time for this? Can the team reach all stakeholders with a presentation or demonstration of what the change will entail? Will this suffice in terms of good communication and open feedback? A contact plan of this sort should tell the team whether the idea is implementable or not. The team now knows whether it is feasible for it to tackle the stakeholders for this particular idea.

Scottish Black Belt

benefits. He would need to be careful about how these were communicated to the stakeholders.

Solution Risk Summary

Just as in the Define stage when the team carried out an evaluation of the risks involved in the project, it is now time to evaluate and prepare action plans to minimize the probability and impact of any risks involved in rolling out the solutions. "No plan ever survived contact with the enemy" is a good watchword here. Getting people to accept new process and changes to how they go about their job can be tricky. It is therefore vital that the team honestly sets down the dangers that they foresee. The risk summary process is the same as in the define phase. What project managers and sponsors should be looking for is a continuous reduction in the level of risk (see Figure 4.7).

Once the team has completed the risk analysis, it is important that the team should summarize the risks and the implications for the project. The team should also check to see that the project risk (the total of the risk scores) to see whether project risk has been reduced through the life of the project. Dave could see that the total risk was lower but he would have preferred it to be even lower.

Communications Plans

At this stage of the project, the team will need to think long and hard about how to communicate the planned changes and the results of the pilot to key stakeholders. The team should go back and update its original stakeholder analysis. It is very important to understand if and how stakeholder views about the project have changed. Dave had asked the

	Solution risks	P	I	Preventive/contingent action	S
A	Sales teams don't take it on-board	5	5	Meeting with Sales Management to ensure complete compliance	A
B	OE/OF Process continues to cause delivery problems	6	4	Need order entry/order fulfillment process review and upgrade	A
C	Suppliers continue to cause delivery problems	7	4	Need Supplier Management involvement to prevent any further issues	A
D	NPI process ineffective	2	3	NPI process is new and working well, needs to be understood, make it part of the general training	
E	Manufacturing process continues to cause delivery problems	5	4	Manufacturing Operations conducting separate Six Sigma program to address issues	
F	Costs escalate, ROI becomes unachievable	3	5	Re-assess costs and ROI; confirm achievable. Also conduct "worst-case-scenario" to determine possible problems	
G	Takes too long to implement, results terminally delayed	6	3	Re-assess timelines for project. Can we do it? If it looks bad then review scope and charter to arrive at something we can do	
H	Other issues eclipse this project, resources redirected by Management	2	8	Discuss with sponsor and senior management. Agree on level of priority this project has and move forwards	A
I	Customers don't like it	2	6	Ensure Customers understand what we're doing and why. Keep them on-board throughout the life of the program. Emphasize the positive impact when complete	
	Total score (out of potential score)	164/900			

Figure 4.7a Risk summary

team to build an outline communications plan. He checked in the Six Sigma best practices database and found an example of a communications plan for another project. The communications plan summary looked at the impact of changes on internal, customer and supplier

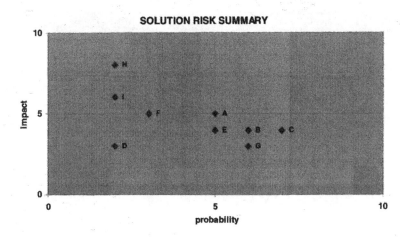

Figure 4.7b Risk summary – continued

Risk summary	Implications for the project
Medium risk. Top three risks: (I) Suppliers continue to cause problems (28). (II) Sales team doesn't take retraining on-board (25). (III) OE/OF process continues to cause delivery problems (24)	Need to manage communications with Sales very carefully

Figure 4.8 Solution risk summary

groups (Figure 4.9). "Let's use this format to develop our plan" he told the team.

Dave had also asked the team to produce a Failure Mode and Effect Analysis (FMEA). He was sure that it would help the stakeholders to see

	Internal groups impacted	Key actions	S
1	Help-desk operations team	Clarify which customer queries are still valid for the telephone Help-desk, and which should be referred to the Help-site	G
2	Sales teams	Ensure they are able to recognize and report revenue from the new "Sales Channel". Help Sales to develop a parallel reporting process	A
3	Customer Care/Accounts Management	Ensure the customer support operations are able to use the new help-site as a tool to increase customer satisfaction, help them sell it	A
4	Web-site design and maintenance teams	Ensure they populate the help-site with the latest and most relevant details, content must be completely up-to-date	A
	Customer groups impacted		
1	IT departments with corporate customers (Europe).	New customer support tool to accelerate resolution of simple issues and to escalate complex issues. Definite positive, customer enhancement	G
2	Small system integrators and re-sellers (Europe).	New customer support tool to accelerate resolution of simple issues and to escalate complex issues. Definite positive, customer enhancement	G
3	Computer kit retailers (UK).	New customer support tool to accelerate resolution of simple issues and to escalate complex issues. Definite positive, customer enhancement	A
	Suppliers impacted		
1	Panic PCBA's Inc.	By 1:1 sessions with Blue Computer supply chain management and by regular technical bulletin. Direct feedback from the customer is due to start, will include more categories of defects, which are to be treated with the same priority settings as before	A
2	Huffy Power Supplies BV	By 1:1 sessions with Blue Computer supply-chain management and by regular technical bulletin. Direct feedback from the customer is due to start, will include more categories of defects, which are to be treated with the same priority settings as before	G

Figure 4.9 Project communications plan

(Process PFMEA)

Customer: Blue Computer (internal)
Process / Product: Helpdesk setup
Process Step: All
Stage No: All

Blue Tag '00401'

Prepared By:
Quality Engineer:
Cust Service Tech:
Web Designer:

Will Buford
Rick Stanley
Dave Clark

Key:
S = Severity
D = Detectability
O = Occurrence probability
RPN = Risk Priority Number

Process Function / Requirements	Class	Potential Failure Mode	Potential Effect(s) of Failure	Potential Cause(s) of Failure / Mechanism	S	O	D	RPN	Current Controls	Recommended Actions	Resp.	Completion Date	Actions taken	S	D	O	RPN
Customer login		Login fails	Customer cannot access help-site	Customer error	9	5	2	90	Customer feedback	Clear login instructions in user-manual	Rick	20-Mar	Manual upgraded	7	4	2	56
				Help-site unavailability	4	4	2	32	Web-site monitoring application	Track server and web-site uptime, instil response measures required.	Will, Dave	23-Mar	Dismissed from server su on team should be OK	3	4	1	12
Reference number logged		Number not supplied	Problem not logged	Customer keying error	5	5	3	75	None	Verify ease of logging in help-site and ref number operations.	Dave	23-Mar	Verified - should be OK	6	3	2	36
		Existing number re-used	Problem confused with another	Customer keying error	3	2	2	12	None	None							
			Problem cannot be escalated	Customer keying error	3	2	2	12	None	None							
Defect resolution track followed		Customer goes off-track	Need to start again	Customer error	2	4	6	48	None	Self-help rules and auto-help start up script.	Dave, Rick	23-Mar	Rules and auto-help reviewed.	2	4	3	24
		Resolution track doesn't resolve problem.	Resolution delayed or completely unsuccessful.	Content error	6	2	1	12	Web-site monitoring application	None.							
'Simpler' defects resolved by Help-site		Problem persists	Need to start again	Customer error	6	4	2	40	None	'Start again' utility and icons added	Dave	23-Mar	'Start again' utility and icons added	3	3	2	18
		Problem migrates	Need to start again	Customer error	4	3	2	24	None	'Start again' utility and icons added	Dave	23-Mar	'Start again' utility and icons added	3	3	2	18
Escalation to telephone help-desk for "harder" problems.		Cannot access Help-desk	Resolution delayed or completely unsuccessful.	Help-desk busy	8	3	2	30	Call waiting monitor	Offer call-back if they wait more than 5 minutes.	Rick, Will	23-Mar	Ongoing action, should be OK but will take time to implement	6	3	1	15
		Reference number doesn't tie up	Resolution delays	Customer keying error	3	5	4	60	Help-desk response and reporting	Help-desk training to handle this issue.	Rick	23-Mar	Training arranged for April	3	4	3	36
		Help-desk cannot resolve problem	Customer dissatisfaction	New problem	7	2	4	56	Failure process and reporting	Interactive 'new problem' log, authorise returning policy.	Rick	22-Mar	New problem log in place OK	5	2	2	20
Connection to Advice and Upgrade Sales centre		Link doesn't work	Customer early log-out	Content error	2	3	3	27	Web-site monitoring application	Web design review.	Will, Dave	23-Mar	Design review planned for 21 April.	3	2	2	12
		Sales pitch ineffective	Sales not achieved	Content inadequate	2	4	2	16	None	None.							
Overall closure, metrics and reporting.		Customer records lost	Metrics and tracking impossible	Customer keying error	6	4	2	48	None	Web design review.	Will, Dave	22-Mar	Design review planned for 21 April.	4	4	2	32

Figure 4.10 Best practices FMEA analysis

that they were approaching the solution implementation with effective plans and contingency plans. The team had not completed a FMEA analysis before so again they looked up the electronic best-practices database.

They then put together their own analysis. Dave was interested to see how the Risk Priority Numbers (RPNs) looked for the project (Figure 4.10). They would have to work through the RPNs for the project after the action plan in the FMEA had been implemented.

Improve Checklist

By the end of the Improve phase, the project team has basically completed its major tasks. The team has set up a position where the improved processes will be implemented and is preparing to hand over control of the new processes to the line managers or process owners who will be responsible for it in the long term. However, first the project team needed to get through the Improve checklist. The Control phase would have to wait until they have achieved sign-off of Improve from the Master Black Belt, Finance and the project sponsor.

Reflections on review meetings

When you sit with a nice girl for two hours it feels like two minutes. When you sit on a hot stove for two minutes it feels like two hours – that's relativity.

Albert Einstein

Dave smiled as Melanie showed him the Einstein quote. He was clearly hoping for a meeting that wasn't a "hot stove"! He knew that the project team had prepared well and had produced an excellent set of outputs (Figure 4.11).

The reviews went well, and both Finance and the MBB signed-off their reviews with only a few questions of clarification. Dave was surprised how well the team's output had stood up to the scrutiny of two very strong and knowledgeable reviewers. However, he also knew that he had a good team using best-practice processes that was very effective at proving its conclusions with fact-based analysis. "None of us would have got through reviews like these before we learned about Six Sigma" Dave had said to the team. "With the Six Sigma approach we have the confidence to make a difference and to make decisions. Finance and the MBB are confident that by applying Six Sigma, we know what we are doing. It is a great win-win for both the team and the reviewers."

Dave's final task in Improve was to take John Kelly through the check-list and to gain final sign-off for Improve. Dave had spent enough time with John to know that he liked the outline solution, but earlier in the phase he had had some doubts about the preferred solutions. Dave had had to work hard to show John that the pilot supported the new pro-cesses and that the business case for the project was now very strong. John looked pleased to see Dave, the relationship between project spon-sor and manager was growing well. It is said that "the basis of trust is confidence." John certainly seemed to be showing real trust in Dave and his project team. He opened his remarks by saying "Dave, when are you going to get this project finished so that you can start the next one and we can spread your team's skills wider in Blue Computers?" It was always more fun to work with John when things were going well!

Dave emerged from John's office three hours later. It had been one of the toughest reviews that he had ever had. John was firm but friendly. He wanted to be absolutely sure that the solution was going to work. He had an interesting tendency to be very direct and to probe any weak-

	Deliverables	Project manager comments	S	Sponsor comments	Y/N
1	*Improvement ideas* – Is there a strong list of improvement ideas?	Strong list, many good ideas from the sales team	G	Excellent	Y
2	*Ideas shortlist* – Have the improvement ideas been properly screened and short-listed?	Yes we have five good ideas with realistic expectation of implementation and of yielding an improvement	G	Excellent	Y
3	*Success criteria* – Is the team's preferred solution based on good success criteria?	Based on expected impact of project, but also on impact (or lack of) from previous projects in the same field	G	I'd like to see this quantified	Y
4	*Buy-in* – Does the solution have the active support of the sponsor and key people who will be impacted?	100% buy-in achieved	G	Excellent	Y
5	*Pilot plan* – Is the pilot and testing approach valid?	Pilot will train two core sales offices to determine impact of adhering to the commit process	G	Enough? Good proposal	Y
6	*Pilot results* – Do the results of the pilot support the improvement targets set out in the goal statement?	Worked well, need to roll it out	G	Yes, move it along	Y
6	*Learning* – Has the solution incorporated key learning from the pilot?	Yes, although the pilot proceeded much as planned	G	Agree	Y
7	*Preferred solution* – Will the preferred solution deliver the improvement targets set out in the goal statement?	Not 100%, needs a Process Improvement Project	A	Agree	N

Figure 4.11

8	*Risk* – Does the roll out plan address potential problem areas with contingency plans?	Yes, the key issues will be addressed, performance improvement is expected in line with outlook	G	Agree	Y
9	*Business case* – Will the proposed solution deliver the business case?	Yes, provided business growth projections are achieved	G	Agree	Y
10	*Updated project plan* – Is the plan for the Control phase robust?	Still behind schedule although considerably closer to original plan than last phase.	G	Plan is robust and appears to have regained some lost time.	Y
11	*Concerns* – Are there any areas of outstanding concern?	Sales team buy-in firming up now. Need a separate internal Process Improvement Project	A	Agree	Y

Master Black Belt sign-off	Date submitted	Date approved	MBB comments	S
Required outputs – Has the project team produced the key outputs to the satisfaction of the MBB?	01-Apr-01	7-Apr-01	All major outputs required for this phase are complete	G

Finance sign-off	Date submitted	Date approved	Finance comments	S
Finance approval – Does Finance support the business case for this project?	01-Apr-01	7-Apr-01	Business case is robust	

Conclusion	Date submitted	Date approved	Sponsor comments	S
Ongoing validity – Is this still a valid project and should it proceed?	08-Apr-01	13-Apr-01	Continue on this course	

nesses in Dave's case from several different angles. One of the project team had once warned Dave about John's directness "Its like lions with wildebeest" he said "It's not personal but when he's hungry he'll look for the weakest spot." John had certainly done that, but then again Dave knew the most challenging sponsors get the best results. That beer was going to taste very very good! John was very pleased with the project team's performance and he had given Dave a special charge number for a project team celebration. "Enjoy yourselves and don't worry about the team evening affecting your project budget" he added just before Dave left. "Control begins on Monday" Dave told the team "I am going to really enjoy having this weekend off – and I suggest you do too."

Dave was called later by John's secretary. John wanted to arrange a lunch time meeting in about two weeks' time. She told Dave that John was reviewing plans for next year and he would appreciate Dave's input on how Six Sigma should be taken forward. Six Sigma was really getting Dave a level of exposure with the senior management team that would not have been possible in the past.

5

The DMAIC Process – Control

Change is only complete when people in the organization adopt a "new way of doing things" as the accepted way of doing things. Unless this happens people may well return to old ways and another improvement initiative simply dies away slowly. The Control phase of the DMAIC process focuses on the wider implementation of the new processes and on sustaining the change.

Objectives of the Control Phase

The objectives of the Control phase are to implement the new processes in all areas of the organization and to put in place robust plans to ensure that the improvement is sustained and financial benefits are delivered. The pilot and the Improve phase proved that the new processes will work and can be implemented in all the planned areas. The main task of

What makes Six Sigma so effective?

Part of what makes Six Sigma so effective and successful is that it is packaged in a way that makes it easy for organizations to implement. A company seeking to apply Six Sigma need not wonder how to get started or how to proceed; the path it must follow is prescribed precisely.

Michael Hammer and Jeff Goding, "Putting Six Sigma in Perspective" (2001)

the Control phase is to "sell" the wider implementation to a wider group of stakeholders and users. It is particularly important to have clear response plans for dealing with the inevitable "teething problems" that can be expected from the wider implementation of new processes.

The outputs of the control phase are:

• Ongoing process management

• Process improvements and control

• Standards and procedures for new processes

• Response plans

• User training in new processes

• Lessons learned

• Team rewards

• The Control phase checklist

Dave Spencer had talked the team through his priorities for the Control phase. "We have a lot to do and we need to get it done efficiently" he told the team "We need to balance our time between implementation planning, handing over the new processes and finalizing the documentation for the project." He was pleased by the response of the team, they were still highly committed and keen to bring the project to a successful conclusion. Dave was going to enjoy working with them and seeing them properly rewarded for their efforts.

Is Six Sigma just another a one-year initiative?

"This is about addressing the DNA of the company. It is a 10-to-15-year commitment." (Jim McNerney, CEO, 3M)

"You don't change a large company all at once. You have to go out unit by unit and get real buy-in from the organization." (Mike Beer, Harvard Business School)

*SMART
PEOPLE
TO HAVE
ON YOUR
SIDE*

Ongoing Process Management

At the end of the Control phase the project team will be disbanded or moved on to other tasks. This can leave functional managers and people nervous and apprehensive about the willingness and ability to adopt and sustain the new processes. After all, they have been used to being able to

---

What is a process owner and what do they do?

A process owner is usually a senior manager with responsibility for the end-to-end performance of a process. The process owner must sign-off the detailed process design and performance parameters. The process owner must also ensure that effective actions are taken if a process moves outside alarm levels or acceptable limits. Most organizations have a loose structure of process ownership. Six Sigma demands that the hierarchy of process ownership is much tighter and managed more proactively.

Scottish Black Belt

*SMART
ANSWERS
TO TOUGH
QUESTIONS*

turn to the Black Belt and their team with concerns. Therefore, it is critical that the project team manage the handover process carefully.

The basis of the handover is a clear set of control measures and alarm levels for the new process owner(s). The alarm levels are designed to signal when things are going outside upper or lower tolerance limits. It should also set out what actions the process owner should instigate if these alarm points are reached.

The implementation of the new processes was going well and to plan. Dave was pleased at the speed with which the team had pulled together the ongoing process management documentation (Figure 5.1). They had identified the key process measures and the targets and alarm levels for the new processes. The team had also identified the appropriate actions that should be taken if alarm levels were exceeded.

Process Improvements and Control

Handovers in large organizations are notoriously difficult to manage effectively. It is too easy to stimulate negative behaviour on both sides. The project team can be seen to be pushing too hard or the new process owner can be reluctant to take on responsibility. The key to effective handovers is balance and trust. The project team needs to handover good processes, implementation plans and documentation. The new

SMART VOICES

I know of no company that took less than six years to achieve a position of quality leadership within their industry. Usually it took closer to ten years.
Joseph Juran, Inside Track (2002)

Ongoing process management details		
Process name	Customer delivery commit process	None
Process purpose	Give an accurate/firm delivery date for any given customer order	None
Review frequency	Weekly and monthly metrics reviews will all touch this	None
Process owner	Hannibal Speaker/Harry Palmer	Current performance levels are still well below the target. Ongoing focus is needed across all departments involved to reach the targets

Key process measures		Performance indicators	P	Target level	Handover level
1	On-time delivery metrics	Ongoing process management	10	Minimum 95% on time	60% on time
2	Predictability metrics	Shipment performance: actual vs. promised	8	Minimum 98% accurate	68% accurately predicted
3	Customer reschedule rates	% orders rescheduled by region monthly	7	Maximum 5% unexpected	24% unplanned/ unexpected
4	Supplier decommit rate	% decommits by Supplier monthly	6	Zero	10%
5	Manufacturing operations decommit rate	% decommits by Manufacturing Operations monthly	5	Zero	15%

Key process measure		Alarm levels	Contingent actions to resolve issues
1	On-time delivery metrics	94% on-time	Monitored by Quality Assurance team, Logistics, QA and Sales conference calls if limit breached
2	Predictability metrics	97% predictable	Monitored by QA team, raise at weekly business review, Sales team conference-in to meeting.
3	Customer reschedule rates	6% unexpected	Sales team to address with customer
4	Supplier decommit rate	More than 1 per month	Supplier management weekly review, action with supplier(s) involved
5	Manufacturing operations decommit rate	More than 1 per month	Manufacturing ops weekly review, action internally, report findings to all

Figure 5.1 Ongoing process management

process owner needs to demonstrate enthusiasm and commitment to the proposed changes.

Training plans are also a key part of the handover process. The project team must ensure that effective training material and plans are in place to build skills in the new processes. Training budgets will also be important. There is no point designing new processes and training materials if there is no budget to pay for the training!

Dave and the team had worked well with Hector Palmer – the new process owner. Hector had initially been somewhat distant, he had seen too many people burned by handovers in the past. However, the thoroughness of the team's work had impressed him and he could see how the new processes were going to work. Hector had also been suspicious about all the Six Sigma jargon; it seemed to be a lot to learn. However, Dave had been good at spending time with him explaining how it worked and taking away some of the mystery of Black Belts, control charts and Six Sigma documentation. They had worked through the handover sign-off document together (Figure 5.2).

Lessons Learned

One of the most valuable but least favourite activities on a project is the process of capturing lessons learned. The reluctance to capture lessons is usually a sign of fatigue with the project, so make the process fun. This can involve a new or more exciting location, maybe offsite or perhaps in a meeting room the team normally doesn't have access to. You may want to bring in a different facilitator or switch some of the roles in the project team. Whatever you do the key is drive out learnings from the project in a format that others can use on their projects.

In simple terms, lessons learned can be of two main types, things that

Process owner	Comments		
Hector Palmer	Sales training has gone well through the pilot stage, rest of EMEA are keen to learn and improve. Supplier management processes and OE/OF process improvement programmes are sorely needed to enhance the overall customer experience and to capitalize on this regime of continuous improvement		
Key process improvements	**"What is to be done differently?"**		**Impact on process performance**
1 Customer delivery commits	Sales team to ensure commit process is complete before informing customer		Customer receives a committed delivery date that has been agreed by the whole organization so it is more realistic and has the support of all.
2 New product availability	Sales team to verify new product availability using system before offering it to the customer		Customer will only be offered new products that are genuinely available.
3 Schedule changes by Operations	Operations to ensure Sales agree schedule changes before accepting them		Operations and Sales agree any internal re-schedule impact before contacting the customer so that there are no surprises.
4 Schedule changes by third-party suppliers	Operations to ensure Sales agree schedule changes before accepting them		Operations, suppliers and Sales agree any supply-base reschedule impact before contacting the customer so that there are no surprises.
Sign-off elements	**Y/N**	**Comments**	
1 Project objectives achieved?	Y	Improvements started immediately, monitoring approach to 95% OTD (latest measure showed improvement from 60% to 83% OTD)	
2 Customer signed-off benefits?	N	Customers verbally happy, still to obtain formal sign-off, need to agree format for this	
3 Documentation complete?	N	Final report-writing in progress, some follow-on into other projects	
4 Stakeholders informed?	Y	All directors signed-off	

Figure 5.2 Process controls and handover

5	Process scorecard established?	Y	Managed through Logistics weekly/monthly/quarterly review forums
6	Handover performance agreed?	Y	All parties happy with handover performance criteria and metrics
7	Project learnings recorded?	Y	Useful learnings on analysis tools for future projects. This has emphasized the need for a process improvement project on the order entry/order management process
8	Reward and recognitions updated?	N	Ongoing discussions on rewards and recognition, will need some of the same people for the OE/OF process improvement project
Final acceptance		**Y/N**	**Comments**
	Hand-over complete?	Y	Flow into OE/OF process improvement project

Figure 5.2 *Continued*

went well and things that did not. Things that went well are easy to identify and discuss. The team should also record if they are best practices to be held on a central database. Things that did not go well are

SMART VOICES

What were the key lessons learned?
- Six Sigma – driven for the top throughout the deployment
- Start with a change management initiative
- Select the right full time resources – training is a major investment
- Leadership skills required to fulfil the jobs – projects deal
- Do not create an élite, it makes it difficult at re-integration time
- Be fair with compensation, but don't overkill
- Measure performance over time
- Listen to the people in the trenches

Dr Heather Farnham, Master Black Belt, Bombardier Aerospace–Shorts

also valuable but often more difficult to discuss. The Black Belt should keep the session "open and honest" so that insights into ways to improve projects can also be captured. Finally, the team should also brainstorm future improvement opportunities. This is a very effective way to keep a company's "hopper" of project ideas current and full.

Dave and the team thoroughly enjoyed the lessons learned session. The session had begun with an "icebreaker" where everyone in the room related their funniest moment on the project. They had then brainstormed the things that had gone well and produced a good list with several best practices. The "what went badly" part of the session started slowly.

Dave got the session moving by contributing his chief failing on the project. Once he started everyone joined in. The session concluded with a great discussion of future improvement and project opportunities. Dave asked the team members to enter several of the ideas on the new "Ideas Generation" software that had just been introduced into Blue Com-

What didn't go so well?
- Difficult when problems cut across divisional/company boundaries
- Inconsistent use of methods – seen as bureaucratic and time wasting
- Limited use of targets and measures
- Lack of prioritization and focus on real customer problems
- Process model not holistic
- Process owners nodding – not doing.

Allan Mees, Standard Life (2002)

SMART VOICES

	What went well?	What are the key lessons to learn?	Best practice?
1	Co-operation between various team members	Early involvement and participation are essential	Y
2	Sales team embraced training	Sell the benefits of change to ensure changes are internalized	N
3	Excellent output from brainstorming produced several unexpected improvements	Should brainstorm more often – make it a regular part of continuous improvement process	Y
4	Two other improvement projects spawned by this one	Maintain the atmosphere of improvement to keep this going	Y
5	Timescale and budgetary requirements were met	Team leader should keep a constant eye on these elements and signal where limits are being reached	N
6	Good/effective/upfront support from senio r management	Value of management involvement reaffirmed, this is the way to do it next time	N
7	Six Sigma raining for team was ideal and highly motivational	Ensure the right training for the right audience is identified and delivered at the right time	Y

	What went badly?	What are the key lessons to learn?	Insights?
1	Project tried to address several large issues	Get the scope right – better with experience	Y
2	Project went in an unanticipated direction	Ensure every option is considered early on, then narrow down to the best solution-options	N
3	Accurate ROI very difficult to reach on a project like this	Discuss methodologies with finance to make ROI as easy for any type of project	Y
4	Sales team inconsistent in their acceptance of the need to re-train	Don't anticipate the breadth or eventual destination of the program	Y
5	Program manager struggled with influencing of and buy-in from some teams/groups	Better training and selection of program managers is essential	N

Figure 5.3 Lessons learned

6	Define and Improve phases slipped schedule	Better planning at outset and better management throughout program	N
	Future process improvement opportunities	Potential impact on performance	
1	Order entry and order fulfilment process should be subject to a similar project	Reduce cycle time and error rates in Operations, faster cash-to-cash	
2	Ongoing supplier development activities needed, along with a review of all supplier contracts	Supplier performance and predictability improved	
3	Sales operations training policies need to be reviewed with HR, are they getting enough?	Sales force response to training was good, very motivational option for the future	

Figure 5.3 *Continued*

puters. "If every project team was producing insights and ideas like this" he told the team "This company is going to make a fortune out of Six Sigma."

Rewarding the Team

One of the best activities on a Six Sigma projects is rewarding people for their contribution. In most companies, this can be a hit-and-miss process. Six Sigma demands a close linkage between rewards and contributions to team and individual targets.

> It's the only program I've ever seen where customers win, employees are engaged in and satisfied by, and shareholders are rewarded. Everyone who touches it wins.
>
> Jack Welch

SMART QUOTES

Individual contribution & rewards statement			
Name	**Time period**	**ICRS coach**	
Kath Taylor	Dec 2000–Jan 2001	Gordon Lightweight	

	Idea number	Idea contributed	Result
1	234	Define and track the $$$ cost of order management	Able to arrive at a real ROI based on tracking document
2	126	Measure the process through the (talked about but never-used) "cash-to-cash" cycle time	A new and effective metric seated in the financial performance of the business

	Project number	Expected project contribution	TT	IT	Comments
1	Fun/D&P/002	To keep the project within budget and to manage any financial or budgetary issues	G	G	Excellent input which helped support the project ongoing justification
2	Fun/D&P/003	To contribute to the overall impact and effectiveness of the project by challenging the financial assumptions	G	G	Good solid and challenging Financial support
3	Fun/D&P/004	To develop new metrics and validate the existing metrics for these processes	G	G	Metrics developed and validated

	Expected rewards	Comments	
1	Level 1 bonus for the quarter as well as contributors bonus at project-end	This is a challenging ICRS; however, expect Kath to rise to the occasion	
2	Additional bonus for demonstration of creativity in areas of metrics and control	Expect Kath to deliver in these areas	

	Areas for future development	Comments	
1	Needs greater exposure to senior management through projects and presentations	Kath needs more experience in working with senior managers, this will help her to develop her decision-making skills	
2	Needs to have a team working for her to stretch her other managerial skills	Kath is ready for this move, involvement in this successful project will enhance her reputation among her peers and develop her self-confidence	

Figure 5.4 Kath Taylor's ICRS

ICRS summary	Individual	S	ICRS coach	Y/N
Is this ICRS stretching but achievable?	Not too stretching, look forward to the metrics development	G	Kath will require help in this area to ensure she delivers	Y
Has this person made a significant personal contribution to project success?	Yes, I have maintained control of the budgetary aspects of the project and have worked through the new metrics	G	Has done a good job and contributed to the project	Y
Has this person made a significant team contribution?	Yes, I have maintained control of the budgetary aspects of the project and have worked through the new metrics	G	Has done a good job and contributed to the project	
Has this person delivered their ICRS?	I believe I have – in all respects	G	Agree – excellent job, ready for a further challenge	Y
What is the agreed performance rating?		G	Top 5% – exceptional	

Figure 5.4 *Continued*

Dave had completed an Individual Contribution and Rewards Statement (ICRS) for each of his project team members. However, he knew that it was important to discuss this with each individual face to face. He knew that performance reviews should always be done in person; the electronic version was a record, not a means of communication! He sat down with Kath Taylor to take her through his comments and to hear her thoughts on the project (see Figure 5.4). He remembered what the Master Black Belt had told him about these reviews. "It's a two way process" he had said "You will learn as much about your strengths and weaknesses as a Black Belt as they will learn about themselves. Give them time to talk, you will not regret it."

The Control Checklist

The Control phase concludes with a checklist. The difference in the Control checklist is the number of people who may be involved in the sign-off process. The key people involved in this sign-off will include the Master Black Belt, process owner, Finance representative and the project sponsor. This level of sign-off may appear excessive but it is critical to bring the project to an agreed conclusion.

The project team had to work hard to meet Dave's deadline for completion of the Control checklist (see Figure 5.5). The process had been complicated because the Finance representative was faced by multiple deadlines from other projects. "It's part of Murphy's law that all projects will converge on the same finish dates" Dave said to John Kelly. "It looks like we may slip by a few days in getting Finance sign-off." John had not been pleased by this latest slippage but he recognized the squeeze on time in Finance. However, the most important thing was to get the right result and this would take a little more time.

Dave emerged from the final project review with a big smile. He was delighted that it had gone so smoothly. He remembered a favourite quote from Winston Churchill "There is nothing more exhilarating than being shot at without result." They had done it. The project had been signed-off as complete. He was truly a Six Sigma Black Belt. They had done it as a team and what a team they had built. He had a group of Green Belts who were now ready to be Black Belts and a group of project rookies who were as good as any Green Belt in the company now. John had muttered something about trying out a Design for Six Sigma (DFSS) project next. Sounded like more Six Sigma training and more challenges on the next project.

	Outputs	Project manager comments	S	Sponsor comments	Y/N
1	*Project delivery* – Is there clear evidence that the goal statement and project charter have been delivered?	Yes, the initial improvements have been met, need to monitor for the next 4–12 weeks to ensure improvement is embedded	G	Agree	Y
2	*Process scorecard* – Is the process scorecard for this solution agreed and documented?	Scorecard under review, draft has been accepted	A	Escalate to push through	Y
3	*Measures* – Are there clear mechanisms in place to provide process scorecard measures?	Yes, new metrics and control charts will provide all the control and data necessary	G	Agree	Y
4	*Documentation* – Are all key documents and analysis recorded in the project data repository, and are the new processes documented and published?	Not all complete	A	Escalate to push through	N
5	*Process owner* – Is there a clearly identified process owner for the new solution and ongoing operations?	Yes (Logistics Director)	G	Under review	Y
6	*Future process improvements* – Has the project team identified areas for future process improvements/refinements for the new process owner?	Not yet formally	A	Need to close this out and move on	N
7	*Troubleshooting* – Are there clear alarms and emergency fixes to support ongoing process management?	Yes, control mechanisms and Operational reviews (weekly) will keep track of any issues and ensure resolution	G	Good	Y
8	*Close-out workshop* – Has the project team conducted a close out workshop, documented key learnings and review external consultant performance?	Close out and lessons learned completed, several members keen to embark on another project	G	Good	Y

Figure 5.5 Control checklist

9	*Recognition* – Has the project team's contributions been recognized and rewarded?	Not yet		Need to close this out and move on	N
10	*Ongoing process control* – Is the plan for the ongoing control robust and feasible?	Yes, control plans and charts	G	Agree	Y
11	*Concerns* – Are there any areas of outstanding concern?	Only those listed above	A	Agree	Y

Master Black Belt approval	Date submitted	Date approved	MBB comments	S
Required outputs – Has the Master Black Belt approved the key project outputs?	01-May-01	02-May-01	Good delivery	G
Process owner approval				
Handover – Has the Process Owner accepted the new processes?	01-May-01	03-May-01	Handover complete	G
Finance approval				
Finance approval – Has Finance signed off the business case and completion of the project?	01-May-01	07-May-01	Good business case	G
Conclusion				
Ongoing validity – Has this project been completed?	03-May-01	08-May-01	Great project, well done	G

6

Successfully Managing Six Sigma Change to Deliver Financial Benefits

In the past, there have been as many successful Six Sigma projects as failures. We know that there is nothing wrong with the method and tools just poor set up and execution. Six Sigma success requires intelligent management of change and an absolute focus on the delivery of financial benefits

SMART QUOTES

Common sense is the collection of prejudices acquired by age eighteen.

Albert Einstein

Introduction

This chapter of the book is focused on two themes; how to manage the change process effectively and how to deliver successful Six Sigma projects and financial results. Much of what you will read is just common sense. Much of what you will need to do to be successful is to apply common sense. Six Sigma is not "rocket science". It is about consistently applying best practices and common sense to common business problems. Remember our initial analysis of the continuous improvement problem – companies are achieving success rates of 20–30% on continuous improvement projects that should have success rates of 90% or above. In this chapter, we return to the factors that can help you to achieve a probability of success of over 90%.

Napoleon's Rules of Strategy

- Adjust the ends to the means at your disposal
- Keep the object always in mind, whilst adapting to circumstances
- Choose the course of least expectation
- Exploit the lines of least resistance
- Ensure that both plans and dispositions are flexible

Why Change Fails and How to Manage for Six Sigma Success

There are many reasons why projects fail. These reasons cover many different areas and they can have complex interrelationships. It is important that all project managers and teams involved in Six Sigma projects should understand the causes of failure and what they have to do to be successful.

Many of these factors are already well known to you and your colleagues. Six Sigma methods can help you to be systematic at eliminating their impact. The important thing about a Six Sigma programme is that it can enable a company to address these areas within a systematic framework. In this chapter, we will work through the common causes of change failure and how Six Sigma can help you to be successful. Let's start by asking you to think about the areas where change management needs most improvement in your company or projects. You should assess where the major strengths and weaknesses are in your company's current approach to change. In the rest of this section, we will discuss how Six Sigma can help to improve each area of change

Dave Spencer had completed his Change Assessment Matrix in the Define phase (see Figure 6.1). He had spent an hour with John Kelly his project sponsor working through the 12 areas. He had found the exercise to be very useful. John had been impressed by the way it forced them both to be open and honest about what would have to be managed. They both wanted the project to be very successful. They had worked out in less than an hour some key areas where they would have to be careful.

Leadership and Vision

No change programme, even if it is Six Sigma, can succeed without clear leadership and vision. Six Sigma demands that senior management commit themselves to initiating and sustaining the programme. There are great examples of Six Sigma leadership and vision in companies like GE, Motorola, 3M and Dow Chemicals. If you want to see real leadership

Change area	Key questions	Score 1= major issues 3 = some issues 5 = no problems	Status (RAG)
Leadership and vision	Is senior management seen to be committed to Six Sigma? Is there a clear vision for continuous improvement?	5	
Change focus	Is there a clear programme for continuous improvement? Is your company as good at finishing projects as starting them?	3	
Company history and culture	Is your history and culture supportive of Six Sigma? Is there significant internal resistance to change?	1	
Planning	Is your company good at planning for change? Are scarce resources being effectively allocated to projects?	3	
Balanced timescales	Will your Six Sigma projects generate enough benefits to be cash positive in this financial year? Is there a good balance between short and longer term change projects?	5	
Project management	Does your company encourage a culture of excellent project management? Do you have a strong cadre of Black Belts and Green Belts?	3	
Team involvement	Are the best project managers overloaded? Is it easy to get people to commit to projects?	5	
Knowledge and sharing	Is knowledge shared effectively in your company? Is it easy to access information on best practices and old projects?	5	
Skills & training	Have people been properly trained to be effective at Six Sigma? Are good tools and techniques available to project teams?	5	
Rewards	Do people feel that their contributions to Six Sigma projects are properly rewarded? Do Black Belts and Green Belts see a clear linkage between their efforts and rewards?	3	
Communications	Are communications about Six Sigma working in your company? Is it easy to find the latest information on Six Sigma progress?	3	
Use of external consultants	Is your company making effective use of external consultants? Are there effective mechanisms for transferring knowledge from external consultants to your employees?	5	

Figure 6.1 Change assessment matrix

Thoughts on leadership

"Leadership is the art of getting someone else to do something you want done because he wants to do it." Dwight D. Eisenhower

"Leadership is a harder job to do than just choose sides. It must bring sides together." Jesse Jackson

"Management is doing things right; leadership is doing the right things." Peter Drucker

and vision look at the web sites and annual reports for these companies. You will come away with no doubt that Six Sigma is part of the culture and DNA of these companies. They encourage commitment by building Six Sigma into everything they do. In many Six Sigma companies, it is mandate that managers are only eligible for bonuses and promotion if they have Six Sigma qualifications.

Dave was pleased with the level of commitment that was being shown by senior management. It was clear that the CEO was behind Six Sigma

Why change fails?	What to do about leadership and vision	Why a Six Sigma approach works?
• Lack of vision	• Clear vision linked to business imperatives	• Clear linkage to business imperatives
• Lack of clear leadership		
• Lack of external insight	• Build in processes that require external insight	• External forces and customer requirements used to drive improvement plans
• Lack of sustained interest		
• Not focused on right priorities	• Visible and sustained leadership	• Management commitment
		• Clear planning processes
		• Visibility of results
		• Linkage of Six Sigma to rewards and promotion

and that it was being effectively promoted as the major change initiative within Blue Computers. Everyone had heard about it, there were Six Sigma posters and handouts all over the company's offices and it was clear that significant budgets were available for training of people and execution of projects.

Change Focus

Too often we see in companies a fragmented approach to change. The lack of a systematic approach leads to too much faith being placed in the latest management fads or solutions. Most companies are good at starting projects, many of which never get finished. Often, the focus on "doing something" means that too many projects start off with the wrong definition and too low a probability of success. Six Sigma can really help to drive a better change focus. It forces much greater discipline into the way that projects are defined and executed. This project discipline is reinforced by the phases and tool gates approach. The use of phase checklists and approvals ensures two success factors; no project

SMART QUOTES

Thoughts on change focus

"We are guiding Honeywell's future by a steadfast focus on our five initiatives — driving growth, improving productivity, generating cash, developing our people, and using our key enablers like Six Sigma and Digitization to support our efforts." David M. Cote, Chairman Honeywell

"Ability is of little account without opportunity." Napoleon Bonaparte

"Obstacles are things a person sees when he takes his eye off his goal." Joseph Crossman

"It is well said, there is nothing wrong in change if it is in the right direction." Winston Churchill

Why change fails?	What to do about change focus?	Why a Six Sigma approach works?
• Too much faith in quick fixes and magic bullets • Start many – finish few • Lack of effective reviews • Fire–aim–ready	• Integrated plan • Systematic methodology • Focus on delivery and light touch reviews • Ready–aim–fire	• Best practice methods built in • Sponsors focused on delivery and results • Checklist and reviews to keep focus

can proceed to a new phase without rigorous scrutiny and projects that get stuck within a phase are identified and dealt with much more quickly.

Dave Spencer had seen many other change initiatives come and go in the past. Business Process Re-engineering, Total Quality Management, Lean Manufacturing, eCommerce had all been magic bullets that were meant to be instant fixes to long-term problems. At least this time Six Sigma seemed to have the right focus and to have set out a realistic perspective on what it was going to take to be successful. "It's great to have a plan that you can believe in and your team can accept" he told John Kelly "it makes a heck of a difference!"

Company History and Culture

Company history and culture can be either a major cause of change success or a major cause of change failure. In GE, it is easy to see that the Six Sigma culture is a major cause for celebration. In many companies, complacency in the history and culture are seen to be major reasons why change fails. Six Sigma helps because it places a strong emphasis on building an effective culture of continuous improvement and current – not past – performance. The building of a strong cadre of Black Belts

Thoughts on company history and culture

"Man are nearly always willing to believe what they wish."   Julius Caesar

"Sacred cows make the best hamburgers."   Mark Twain

"Success makes you dumb, real success makes you really dumb."

Gary Hamel

and Green Belts also helps to build a strong team of good project managers who have the confidence and ability to make change happen.

Dave knew that Six Sigma was a very powerful method. He also knew that the culture of the company could throw up some significant obstacles. Dealing with the sales organization was not going to be simple. They had their own views and they had a rewards system that drove their behavior. "We are going to have some interesting discussions with Sales" he told John, "We are going to need some strong facts to get a good result."

Why change fails?	What to do about company history and culture	Why a Six Sigma approach works?
• Legacy of change culture • Complacency • Internal resistance	• Focus on future potential • Focus on opportunity and delivery successes • Involve resistors early	• Focus on ideas, project priorities and business cases • Clearly identifies who is and isn't involved • Makes successes visible to all

Planning

Too many companies are reluctant to apply rigorous planning processes to their change programme. As a result, too much is left to chance. Six

Thoughts on planning

"Well don't worry about it. It's nothing."
Lt. Kermit Tyler, Duty Officer Pearl Harbor, 7 December 1941

"If one does not know to which port one is sailing, no wind is favourable."
Seneca

Sigma companies tend to adopt a different approach. At GE, the annual planning processes are clearly set out on a month by month basis. People in GE know what they have to do and when. This type of planning framework reduces unnecessary uncertainty and helps to breed confidence among project sponsors, managers and teams. The culture of planning is also present at the portfolio and project level in Six Sigma. Project Charters are a good example of how Six Sigma uses clear planning documents to drive success. There is no excuse for poor planning. Six Sigma encourages better planning and provides few hiding places for those that do not want to plan for success.

Dave had enjoyed learning about planning techniques. He realized that in the past he had left too many things to chance. He had caused delays

Why change fails?	What to do about planning	Why a Six Sigma approach works?
• Poor planning and preparation • Poor definition of projects • Poor allocation of resources • Only planning for the expected having to divert committed resources to deal with the unexpected	• Plan, Plan, Plan • Define projects clearly upfront • Allocate scarce resources carefully • Be prepared for the unexpected	• Can't proceed without good plans • Project definition locked in • Resource allocation and balancing mechanisms • Plans for the expected but retains flexibility to manage unexpected

in projects because he had not been on top of his required actions. Meetings had been delayed, reviews postponed and tasks had been undertaken out of the correct sequence. He smiled when he thought about how unprofessional he would have looked to a good project manager. Then again, the lack of a good planning system had meant that no one had really noticed. "Everyone operated in a cycle of crisis management and we were very good at it" he told the team "The problem is that had we been good planners, most of the crises would have been unnecessary."

Balanced Timescales

In our lives, we can all see the value and impact of timing. We have all been in a meeting where someone's timing has either been spectacularly good or bad. We all enjoy watching a comedian, politician or presenter with good timing. Change programmes are no different – timing is critical. Some companies are committed to change programmes where the benefits are simply too far in the future. Other companies become far too short-term focused, experts in cutting costs but leaving too little opportunity for future competitive success. Six Sigma is a strong methodology for getting people focused on the right things and for achieving a balance between short-term successes and longer-term competitive

Thoughts on balanced timescales

"It changes everybody's lives in the first year. We are betting our performance on Six Sigma. This is something that, if 6 sigma doesn't succeed, the company doesn't succeed."   W. James McNerney, Jr, CEO, 3M

"Strike while the iron is hot, but make it hot by striking."   Oliver Cromwell

Why change fails?	What to do about balancing timescales?	Why a Six Sigma approach works?
• Goals too far ahead • Lack of balance over short and medium term	• Set short-term goals • Balanced delivery of benefits over short, medium and long term	• Balanced portfolio of short- and medium-term projects • Clarity about short-term goals and delivery expectations

advantage. Six Sigma success at continuous improvement is an excellent way of generating the benefits that can be invested in future capabilities. In our experience, there is a close linkage between companies that are good at continuous improvement of their core business and companies that are a capable of delivering genuine and sustainable business innovation. Six Sigma helps to balance the allocation of resources between the short and longer term. It helps to create the spare capacity to pay for the future growth of the company.

Dave really liked the way that Six Sigma forces you to think about the financial benefits that could be delivered this year. "It creates a real discipline among the Black Belts" he told John "You know that your job is to identify opportunities and projects that will deliver this year. You will not find Black Belts proposing projects that have a three year payback. They know that there is still plenty of "low hanging fruit" if you know how to manage projects."

Project Management

Project management is the basic discipline of change success. Too often companies pay too little attention to the value of good project management. They place too little value on their project managers and fail to develop this very valuable resource to anything like the required scale

Thoughts on project management

"The secret of getting ahead is getting started. The secret of getting started is breaking your complex overwhelming tasks into small, manageable tasks and then starting on the first one." Mark Twain

"Real heroes are men who fall and fail and are flawed, but win out in the end because they've stayed true to their ideals and beliefs and commitments." Kevin Costner

and skills level. If you ever want to see the value that smart organizations place on project management skills, then look at a major management consulting company. They are in the business of change. They have large numbers of trained and trainee project managers and they recognize their value constantly. Six Sigma is a method that is based around the "cult of the project manager." It can be seen as a way of bringing the value that external consultants place on project management skills inside your company.

Dave mused on how attitudes to project management had changed over the last 10 years. "It used to be that it was seen as an engineers' tool. Today, it is increasingly seen as a fundamental business and team management method." He told John Kelly.

Dave now had a real sense that they were starting to build a good cadre of project managers. He knew that there was nothing worse in a company than seeing senior management always bringing in external project managers when there was a tough project to deliver. "It was the lack of trust that always use to get to us" he told a friend "It felt like every time there was something that they really wanted to happen, we were not trusted to be good enough." He was fed up with watching all the knowledge and experience from the best projects leave with the external consultants. "They have some really impressive project managers and

Why change fails?	What to do about project management ?	Why a Six Sigma approach works?
• Not enough good project managers • No internal mechanisms for developing sufficient numbers of project managers • Lack of sharing of best practices in project management	• Increase number of good project managers • Develop larger numbers of project managers through successful delivery of the smaller projects	• Uses smaller projects to develop good project managers • Project prioritization and gate reviews • Best practices built in • Targeted use of experts to help solve difficult problems • Recognizes and rewards effective project managers

we trained them!" He knew that Six Sigma had already changed attitudes to project management in Blue Computers.

Team Involvement

Six Sigma is a method that demands team involvement. There are no places on the sidelines for Black Belts and Green Belts; they are committed to the project, not just involved. The objective of Six Sigma training and methods is to ensure that a much greater number of people in a company are capable of making a significant contribution. In too many companies, too much is left to the few to do. The result is overload and inertia. Good people never say no when asked to take on new assignments. However, this mixture of over-ambition and over-optimism is the downfall of many of your best people. Overloaded people don't deliver to plan and they often find it difficult to delegate to others because they have no time to think. It is no fun working for overloaded people, they have too many stresses and too little time to explain things clearly.

"If you are in, you are in!" Dave had told the team. He wanted the whole team to know that this was not going to be a project where people could decide how far to be involved. He wanted a fair sharing of project tasks and a culture of delivering promises. Six Sigma was a real help because there was a clear breakdown of tasks and the phase check-

Why change fails?	What to do about team involvement?	Why a Six Sigma approach works?
• Fragmented • Overload of best • Under load of many people	• Maximizes project team involvement • Balanced allocation of work loads across teams • Surround problems quickly and solve as a team	• Clear monitoring of involvement • Balances workloads and highlights over stretch • Enables teams to surround problems on line, and rapidly • Allows external experts to help

lists made it very clear up front what work was required. He had liked a comment that he had heard from a visiting CEO "There are always problems so what you need is a culture where your people surround problems and solve them as a team. You may not have all the answers at the beginning, but you have a bunch of people who can figure it out together."

Knowledge and Best Practices

Organizations are stuffed full of knowledge. They generally have lots of large databases that store that knowledge. They also have increasingly sophisticated search engines to view that knowledge. However, there is often nothing more difficult to do than to find out what your company already knows. This problem is often caused by several factors:

- People are not good at synthesizing their learning, what they record is too large to be useful

- Personal computers hide and fragment your company's knowledge across thousand of individual and inaccessible hard drives

- Software programmes hide knowledge within files such as Microsoft Word and PowerPoint. You just can't see inside the files without opening them

"Some drink deeply from the river of knowledge. Others only gargle."
Woody Allen

"Water, water, everywhere, and all the boards did shrink; Water, water, everywhere, nor any drop to drink."
Samuel Taylor Coleridge, *The Ancient Mariner*

SMART QUOTES

- People are rarely rewarded for making knowledge available and accessible

The result is that it is often quicker to reinvent than to learn. Smart organizations have recognized this problem and they are using Six Sigma and related software products to open up the best knowledge in their company to their project teams.

Dave recognized that it had been difficult to access project learnings in the past. However, he was determined two things would happen on his project. Firstly, they would make good use of previous projects by ensuring that they got hold of the project documents and project managers from related Blue Computers projects. Secondly, he had decided to record the project documents on a central computer system using a common set of best-practice templates. The system was web based and his team could access it 24 hours a day, 7 days a week. "There will be only one version" he told the team "So we cannot have version control issues. The web based software is easy to access and simple to use. Your job is to synthesize our key insights and learnings. Any of the larger analysis files we will attach to the project file." Things had come a long way since Dave's first project, by automating Six Sigma tools much

Why change fails?	What to do about knowledge sharing?	Why a Six Sigma approach works?
• Not shared • Not accessible • Owned and kept by external consultants	• Shared • Accessible • Easy to use • Easy to share lessons learned	• Knowledge base of projects, best practices and insights • Enabling tools improve productivity and efficiency. Accessible 24×7 over the web • Easy to use mechanisms for sharing lessons learned

more time was spent doing the required work rather than working out how to record it.

Skills and Training

Most companies have too few experienced and confident project managers and teams working on their change projects. This lack of skill results in a lack of confidence between project sponsors, managers and their teams. The uncertainty about skills and capabilities leads to mistrust, reinvention of methods and double guessing about requirements. Six Sigma is clear about the skills and training needs of all the people involved in the programme. Black Belts are trained to be robust project managers. Green Belts are trained to support them either as project managers or as team members. Project sponsors are made aware of the roles and responsibilities. Many Six Sigma companies have trained as many as 1% of their people in Six Sigma tools and techniques. You never hear their people regretting this investment in skills and training.

"If I have ever made any valuable discoveries, it has been owing more to patient attention, than any other talent." Isaac Newton

"I am always ready to learn although I do not always like to be taught."
Winston Churchill

"I never let schooling interfere with my education." Mark Twain

SMART QUOTES

Dave didn't feel he needed to add much about skills and training because that was one of the key strengths of Six Sigma. The training programme integrated skills building with a clear implementation programme. Dave had been on of the first wave of Six Sigma Black

Why change fails?	What to do about skills and training?	Why a Six Sigma approach works?
• Ill-prepared people • No project specific training • Lack of understanding of project methods	• Train people with specific and relevant skills • Make tools and methods easy and fun to use	• Self-development training built in • Easy access to many analytical tools and worked examples • Easy access to best practices

Belts. They were now in the second wave with the third wave planned for later in the year. Dave's latest concern was a personal one, how long was it before he could become a Master Black Belt?

Dave reflected that what were currently Black Belt and Green Belt skills would, over time become standard for all managers in Blue Computers. "Then we really would be cooking with gas!" he thought.

Rewards

As with every initiative, we backed it up with our rewards system. We changed our incentive compensation plan for the entire company so that 60% of the bonus was based on financials and 40% on Six Sigma results. In February, we focused our stock option grants on employees who were in Black Belt training.

Jack Welch

"What gets measured, gets done" goes the saying and it is very true most of the time. Too many companies have a poor linkage between the contribution that they expect from their managers of change and their rewards. This lack of clarity breeds problems. People will only show long term commitment to change if they can see how their contribution is being recognized and rewarded. Six Sigma is highly effective at creating and reinforcing this linkage. Some argue that "being a Black Belt is reward enough". GE has been very clear about the nature of rewards and Six Sigma contributions. There are no rewards that are not Six Sigma related!

Dave had been very up front with John Kelly about rewards – "I need to be able to tell the team about what is in it for them." He had met a Master Black Belt who had failed on a recent assignment because no one in his team had any part of their bonuses tied to the project. The MBB had said "They were very polite and they wanted me to be successful but they had other targets to achieve to get paid! We missed all our major

Why change fails?	What to do about rewards?	Why a Six Sigma approach works?
• Not aligned to objectives • Lack of effective linkages to objectives	• Clear rewards for delivery • Linked to objectives • Effective feedback	• Clear linkages between contribution and rewards • Individual and team targets and rewards identified early • Recognition and rewards built into the process

deadlines and then senior management cancelled Six Sigma because it didn't work. They couldn't see that people had no incentive to make it work." Dave was determined that this would not happen to his project.

Communications

Strategic plan
- Maintain and grow the savings
- Align Six Sigma to company business priorities
- Identify functional priorities and key supporting processes
- Map and baseline key processes
- Identify and carry out Six Sigma projects for current year.

Dr Heather Farnham, Master Black Belt, Bombardier Aerospace–Shorts 2002

It is not easy to be a good communicator. It is not easy to communicate with all stakeholders in a programme of change. Communications is an inexact science. But it is an area when you will know quickly if you are not getting it right! Dave remembered some advice from his Black

Why change fails?	What to do about communications?	Why a Six Sigma approach works?
• Poor communications • Difficult to communicate progress	• Easy to communicate • Easy to find latest information	• All key data in one place for Six Sigma • Relevant data easy to access over the web • Latest data all in one place • Easy to use communications

Belt course – "Communicate, communicate, communicate!" He had appointed one of his Green Belts to be in charge of a weekly communications sheet and to manage the communications plan. "Whatever happens" he had told her "Just keep reminding me about what we need to be communicating to whom."

Use of external consultants

The best external consultancies are "unbelievable warehouses of impressive talent". They have some of the best thought leaders and project managers you will ever meet. They have people who know how to make the right projects happen. But they are not your people and they are too expensive to use on most small, continuous-improvement projects. Your company needs to be very good at managing external consultants. If you know how and when to use external consultants, you will save your company a lot of money and deliver some very impressive financial benefits. Most companies demand knowledge transfer from their advisers, few are good at implementing this aspiration. Six Sigma is a great methodology for improving the relationship between companies

Why change fails?	What to do about external consultants?	Why a Six Sigma approach works?
• Too dominant	• Use "externals" only on the right type of projects	• Clear definition of projects and need for external support
• Internal resistance to outsiders and resentment of status	• Link rewards to success	• Visibility of supplier performance
• Different incentives for success	• Manage costs down constantly	• Visibility of cross-project costs and performance
• Fragmented management	• Secure knowledge internally	• Capturing in-house of project knowledge and learnings

and their external advisers. It focuses internal attention on building a cadre of good project managers. It focuses attention on internal knowledge sharing and ideas creation. It ensures that the company does what it is good at and it uses external consultants to fill genuine gaps in capability. The best relationships between companies and external advisers are mutual respect. The worst are based on unnecessary dependencies.

Thoughts on external consultants

"Don't walk in front of me; I may not follow. Don't walk behind me; I may not lead. Just walk beside me and be my friend."   Albert Camus

Dave was pleased by the new approach that he saw the company taking to external consultants. He had long felt that they were not being managed properly but it was difficult to challenge them. Six Sigma was giving Blue Computers a new faith in the ability of its people. There was growing confidence that internal people could take on tasks that had typically been done by consultants in the past. This had several benefits: it cost less, the benefits came faster and the learning was captured inside the company. Dave also felt that there was a growing pride within the company that it could solve its own continuous-improvement problems.

Project Scorecards and Financial Results

At the end of the day, the success or failure of Six Sigma comes down to financial results. Do not let anyone tell you otherwise. The leading proponents of Six Sigma are very clear about the delivery of financial benefits and the culture of excellence that that creates. In this section of

"We went from 3,000 Six Sigma projects in 1996 to 6,000 in 1997, when we achieved $320 million in productivity gains and profits, more than double our original goal of $150 million. By 1998, we had generated $750 million in Six Sigma savings over and above our investment and would get $1.5 billion in savings the next year."   Jack Welch

"Our focus today is on financial discipline and delivering superior service and products to clients."

William B. Harrison, Jr, Chairman and CEO, J.P. Morgan Chase and Co.

the book, we will look at how companies can monitor and manage the delivery of Six Sigma projects and their financial results. The challenge is one of showing how your project can and will impact today's financial numbers. Part of this challenge involves proving there is a "cause and effect" relationship between new processes and financial benefits. The other challenge is in keeping genuine benefits as benefits. For instance, quite often a saving within a budget (particularly if it is a procurement saving) is simply recognized as an opportunity to spend more money in another area of the business.

Six Sigma Project Progress and Risk Summary

Project progress reporting is important for all Six Sigma projects. At a very basic level, project progress against plan should be monitored through one or two weekly project reports and tollgate reviews at the end of each phase. Some project sponsors like using weekly project reports because they believe that it helps to maintain momentum in project teams. Other people claim that it forces the project manager to spend too much time reporting rather than doing. (You can avoid the unnecessary bureaucracy of one or two weekly reports by having a dynamic web-based reporting system such as Continuous Innovation Culture's Six Sigma software. This type of solution is much more elegant but requires cultural changes.) Progress reporting should focus on making sure that project progress targets are being met and that risk is being managed effectively.

John Kelly and Dave Spencer had agreed that they would start off with weekly project reports using the format shown in Figure 6.2. John was very keen to watch the changes in the project risk summary. He knew that there were going to be issues with Sales and he wanted to know when this was impacting project risks.

The other part of the weekly project reports followed a simple framework of:

• Activities and outputs over the last week

• Planned activities and outputs over the next week

• Issues for management attention

• Changes in the risk summary

• Required management actions.

Dave hoped that they would be able to move off from weekly reports to dynamic on-line reporting as quickly as possible. He knew it would take a little time for John to gain confidence in using web-based Six Sigma software. However, he knew John would try it out.

Project name	Project sponsor	Project manager	Reference
Delivery Predictability	John Kelly	Dave Spencer	DP002

Progress approvals against schedule

Project dates	Start	Original target	Latest forecast	S	Actual	Comments
Authorization					1 Jan	
Define	1 Jan	31 Jan	7 Feb		7 Feb	1 week slippage, authorizing manager off-site
Measure & Analyse	1 Feb	28 Feb	1 Mar		1 Mar	
Improve	1 Mar	31 Mar	13 Apr		13 Apr	2 week slippage
Control	1 Apr	30 Apr	8 May		8 May	

Project risk management summary

Process	Expected risk score	Actual risk score	Actions required	S
Define	200	173		
Measure & Analyse	175	168	Need to reduce risk faster	
Improve	150	140		
Control	100	90		

Figure 6.2 Weekly project report

Six Sigma Project Financials

All Six Sigma projects will start out with a target for financial benefits and then build a detailed business case for the proposed changes. This business case will become more robust as the project moves through the phases. It should be very robust by the end of the Improve phase. A business case will generally be an Excel workbook that contains a detailed analysis of the financials and the assumptions and data that drives the numbers. It should also contain and some level of sensitivity analysis that will identify which changes to the numbers have the most impact on the robustness of the business case.

Business case spreadsheets are not as difficult to create as they look. The approach is fairly standard and people can become more efficient if they take advantage of company standard business case templates. It is always a good idea to have someone working on the business case who has done it before. It saves time and pain! The project manager and team must all understand the business case, it is not just for the guy from Finance.

The Finance function will generally be required to check the business case so it is important that their representatives are involved at an early stage of the project. It is a best practice that a Finance representative should sign-off the phase checklists in Measure & Analyse, Improve and Control. Finance may review the project team's work but it can also be a great help. Use Finance to get access to financial numbers, check assumptions and provide any internal financial benchmarks about other areas of the business.

The business case is a detailed financial document that is not designed for project or portfolio reporting. Within a project scorecard there needs to be a summary of the business case that sets out the key financials. Some companies may also want headcount impact to be reported in this summary. These summary financials should also include assumptions and analysis of factors such as hurdle rates, NPV, IRR and Payback. These measures are used by senior managers as "quick and dirty" summaries of financial numbers. Use them because senior management will always look for them.

Any project is likely to have different types of benefits with different

Where can we expect to find hard financial benefits?

Look in the following areas:

- Lower costs in manufacturing
- Lower sales costs
- Lower administration costs
- Lower procurement costs
- Lower service and returns costs
- Working capital reduction
- Improved cash flow
- Increased product margins
- Faster order to cash cycles
- Headcount reduction
- Headcount avoidance
- Revenue growth
- New revenue from new customers/markets

levels of confidence applying to their delivery. A financial reporting system should identify the different types of benefits (e.g. operating cost, capital cost, headcount reduction, cost avoidance, margin improvement, sales growth) and attach a likely level and probability. As a project progresses, the level of confidence in estimates should reduce from ±50% to ±10%. This is a good guide for forecasting of financial costs and benefits.

Depending on the reporting system, you may want to have a difference between the business case numbers and the financials that the project declares to the portfolio managers. The reason for this is that business case numbers may fluctuate in the early stages of a project. This fluctuation is not helpful if it impacts overall portfolio numbers. You are often better off declaring summary targets and waiting until the business case stabilizes before updating the forecasted costs and benefits. Sharp movements in projected benefits and costs can undermine management confidence in your project. As a project manager, wait until you have confidence in the financials before changing initial forecasts.

At a portfolio level, Six Sigma should enable a company to get a clear view of the likely financial benefits that will be delivered this year and in subsequent years by Six Sigma. The phase and toll gate approach means that forecasted costs and benefits should be visible to senior management throughout a financial year. There should be no big surprises at the end of a financial year. Six Sigma will help to give management predictability over financial benefits particularly if the Six Sigma programme uses an integrated project reporting and tracking system.

Dave had some examples of financial reporting templates that the Master Black Belt had given him – see Figure 6.3.

SMART
ANSWERS
TO TOUGH
QUESTIONS

How does Six Sigma fit with balanced scorecard?

The Balanced Business Scorecard (BBS) was first developed in the late 1980s to provide a richer set of management performance indicators covering areas such as customers, operations, finance, employees and innovation. The BBS concept was designed to create a balanced set of objectives and measures that could be cascaded down from the top to the bottom of a company. Six Sigma success also requires detailed performance measures and data. Many companies have their own scorecards for Six Sigma projects. These are most effective where they apply the principles of the balanced business scorecard in combining financial and non-financial measures. Scorecards can allow summary reporting and drill down reporting capabilities. This requires common standards of recording data and effective project and process disciplines.

Financial projections							
3-year cost–benefit	Quarter 1	Quarter 2	Quarter 3	Quarter 4	Year 1	Year 2	Year 3	Total
Capital costs								
Operating costs								
Operating benefits								
TOTAL								

Benefits area	Benefits delivered	Sponsor comments	S

Rolled up project cost benefits (approved for inclusion in overall portfolio financials)					
Timing	Expected ongoing benefits	Expected one off benefits	Expected operating costs	Expected capital costs	Total	S
This Financial Year						
Future Financial Years						
Total						

Figure 6.3

Six Sigma Project Health Check

The Project Health Check is a simple mechanism that is designed to monitor progress and to keep the project manager and team focused on doing the right projects in the right way. It consists of eight questions that the project manager should ask the team on a regular basis. Each question is scored out of ten. The format allows the project team to see the results on a spider chart. The expectation is that as the project progresses than the overall score should improve. Where there are significant changes downwards in a single score or the overall Project Health Check, then the project sponsor and project manager should take corrective action quickly.

Figure 6.4 shows Dave Spencer's score half way through the Measure & Analyse phases. He is showing concern that not all the critical decisions required are being taken and some uncertainty about financial targets. However, his overall score is higher than his previous Health Check with the project team.

The team liked the Project Health Check. It gave them an opportunity to highlight concerns and to get them discussed. If something wasn't right then it was a good way to identify the problem and solve it fast.

Dave had used the health check and project scorecard to keep focused on the delivery of benefits from the project. He knew that the success of the overall Six Sigma programme would depend directly on the ability of Black Belts to deliver financial success. He had gradually built up John and the team's confidence in the scorecard as the key measurement mechanism. He knew this was critical particularly to proving to John that he had earned this year's performance bonus.

Project success factors		S	Project health check
	Is this project the right project?	9	
	Are target financial benefits realistic and achievable?	5	
	Is this the right team? Are team members available?	9	
	Are stakeholders supportive?	4	
	Can the project deliver within budget?	10	
	Can the project deliver on time?	10	
	Are critical decisions being taken?	3	
	Have all major risks have been identified and managed?	8	
	Current project status	73°₀	
	Overall project status for the last period	66°₀	

Black Belt comments

1	Scores improving
2	Need more access to the project sponsor and to decision makers in Sales
3	Need to watch target financial benefits

Figure 6.4 Project Health Check

7

Introducing Design for Six Sigma (DFSS)

There will be times when continuous improvement through the DMAIC
process will not be enough to raise sigma levels to required standards.
What will be needed is a radically new process. Design for Six Sigma or
DFSS is the Six Sigma method for radical process innovation

Introducing DFSS

It would be wrong to try and describe the whole
methodology for Design for Six Sigma (DFSS) in
one chapter. There is at least another book's worth
of material in DFSS. In this chapter, we will take you
through the major differences between the DMAIC
and DFSS project processes. The first question to
clarify in your mind about DFSS is "Why do we

SMART QUOTES

You can't solve a problem
with the same thinking that
created it.

Albert Einstein

How to turn your customers into innovators

Five steps:

1. Develop a user-friendly tool kit for customers.

2. Increase the flexibility of your production processes.

3. Carefully select the first customers to use the tool kit.

4. Evolve your tool kit continually and rapidly to satisfy your leading-edge customers.

5. Adapt your business practices accordingly.

Stefan Thomke and Eric von Hippel, *Harvard Business Review*, April 2002

need it? Won't DMAIC do for all Six Sigma projects?" By now, you will have realized that you will need DFSS and what you need to know is why. Put simply, DMAIC is a method for projects that are aimed at an incremental improvement in performance. DFSS is a method that is used when incremental improvement is not enough or there is no existing process to improve. DFSS is used for radical or new process innovation.

Different Approaches to DFSS

Whilst DMAIC is generally accepted as the best method for continuous improvement, DFSS has spawned a number of different approaches:

- DMADV (Define, Measure, Analyse, Design, Verify) This is the most commonly seen DFSS method/

- DMADIC (Define, Measure, Analyze, Design, Implement, Control)

This is a method that adds a Design phase into DMAIC and focuses more on implementation.

• DMEDI (Define, Measure, Explore, Design, Implement) This is a method used by companies like Caterpillar and Price Waterhouse Coopers (now IBM).

• IDOV (Identify, Design, Optimize and Verify).

As you can see, there are strong similarities between DFSS methodologies and between DFSS and DMAIC. Many of the tools used in DFSS and DMAIC are the same, but you will often see the more advanced Six Sigma tools being used in DFSS projects.

How DFSS differs from DMAIC

DFSS differs from DMAIC is a number of keys ways. The reason for this is that there has to be a stronger emphasis on new process design. In the early stages of a DFSS project this means stronger focus on customer requirements (and the use of more complex analysis tools such as Quality Function Deployment [QFD]). Measure & Analyse is broadly similar to DMAIC except you can expect to see more exploring and use of computer based process simulation in DFSS. Design is a new area in DFSS and very different to DMAIC. DFSS and DMAIC projects have many similarities on completion, with the need for wide spread implementa-

Why don't we just focus on cost cutting?

A good answer to this comes from Sullivan and Harper's book *Hope is Not a Method* about what they describe as the Management Treadmill. They say:

> "At some point, neither speed nor quality is a sustainable competitive advantage. Cost cutting as an end in itself is worst of all because it merely forces the old engine to labor harder and harder. To be effective, change must be substantive – it must add value and contribute to the long run health of the organization. When unaccompanied by real change, cost cutting is all pain and no gain."

tion and handover of new processes to new process owners. As with all projects, there need to be effective and efficient methods for recording lessons learned and rewarding a successful project team.

Stronger Focus on Customer Requirements in Define

In DFSS, the project team is starting off with an assumption that they cannot fix a current or non-existent process. They need to invent a new one. So the Voice of the Customer becomes even more important than it was in DMAIC. Put simply, DFSS offers a great opportunity to design new processes around the identified needs of customers.

Voice of the Customer and Critical to Quality analysis can be used just as in DMAIC. In addition to these tools, there are others such as QFD and Kano analysis. These tools are more rigorous in their analysis and conclusions. They come out of the Japanese school of quality management techniques. These tools were developed in Japan because of a pressing need to understand the detailed customer requirements of non-Japanese businesses and consumers.

The Define phase in DFSS is similar to DMAIC but with greater use of customer data and surveys. The Define checklist in DFSS is very similar to DMAIC but with greater emphasis on customer needs and new product/service development opportunities. Remember to think about what customer-valued requirements you can build in, and what customer problems you can design out of your product or service.

Adapting the Measure & Analyse Phases in DFSS

The Measure & Analyse phases of DFSS continue with a greater focus on customer requirements. This is likely to include more work on identifying critical customer requirements by segment. Where data does not exist, it will need to be collected by the DFSS project team. Best practices and benchmarking will for a key part of these phases. The Analyse phase is about understanding detailed customer requirements and options for fulfilling these requirements. By the end of the Measure & Analyse phases, the project team should have a good view of the new concept that will be required by customers. They should also have a clear view on the outline "target costing" that will be required in the Design phase.

DM: Do you feel you've learnt by your mistakes here?
PC: I think I have, yes, and I think I can probably repeat them almost perfectly. I know my mistakes inside out.

Peter Cook and Dudley Moore, "The Frog and Peach"

In these phases, the project team will make use of a variety of Six Sigma tools including:

• Best practices and benchmarking

• Kano analysis

• QFD

• Failure Modes and Effect Analysis (FMEA)

• Issues or CTQ trees

• Customer surveys

• Interview workbooks

• Process maps and simulation models

• Brainstorming and affinity diagrams

The team is now ready for the challenges of the Design phase.

The Design Phase

The Design phase is the opportunity to create real process or product innovation. The type of innovation will depend on the nature of the problem that the DFSS project is trying to solve. The start point for the Design phase is a set of concepts and options to be tested. The team takes the design requirements and tests out which elements of the design are most effective. Their task is to deliver a high-level process design. This is likely to include process maps, simulation models, prototypes and a pilot. Tools used in this phase will include:

- Design of Experiments (DOE)/Taguchi design

- Response surface methodology

- Process simulation

Systematic innovation means monitoring seven sources for innovative opportunity:

- The unexpected – the unexpected success, the unexpected failure, the unexpected outside event;

- The incongruity – between reality as it actually is and reality as it is assumed to be or as it 'ought to be';

- Innovation based on process need;

- Changes in the industry structure or market structure that catch everyone unawares.

- Demographics;

- Changes in perception, mood and meaning;

- New knowledge, both scientific and non-scientific.

Peter F. Drucker. *Innovation and Entrepreneurship* (1985)

SMART
PEOPLE
TO HAVE
ON YOUR
SIDE

- Design analysis matrix

- Risk analysis and sometimes HAZOPs

- FMEA

- Pilot plan and test plan

By the end of the Design phase, the project team will be required to go through the Design Checklist. Figure 7.1 gives an example of a Design Checklist from another project in Blue Computers. The project team needs approvals for their work from an experienced Master Black Belt, Finance and the project sponsor.

Implementation and Control in DFSS

In the Implementation and Control phases of DFSS, the project team extends the pilot to a full-scale implementation of the new products or services. The proposed design needs to be validated and implemented on a wider scale. The Implement and Control phases require greater rigor than in DMAIC because of the level of innovation in the products/services. All the handover and control activities required in DMAIC are multiplied in DFSS. Tools that a project team can expect to use in Implement and Control include:

- Control and run charts

- Process management charts

- FMEA

- Risk analysis

- Handover processes

The completion of a DFSS project will require

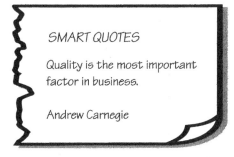

SMART QUOTES

Quality is the most important factor in business.

Andrew Carnegie

Deliverables	Project manager comments	S	Sponsor comments	Y/N
1	*Design ideas* – Is there a strong list of process design ideas?	Idea are strong and varied	G	Ensure we land on the right 2 or 3 to take the project forwards	Y
2	*Design shortlist* – Have the process design ideas been properly screened and short listed?	Shortlist complete, want to review one last time	A	OK, but need to keep momentum up, cannot afford further slippage	Y
3	*Success criteria* – Is the team's preferred design based on good success criteria?	Yes, based on reduction in help cycle time and in traffic through telephone helpdesk.	G	Are we sure these are all the success criteria? What about reliability and hit rates?	Y
4	*Buy-in* – Does the design have the active support of the sponsor and key people who will be impacted?	Yes by in is assured	G	Agree	Y
5	*Pilot plan* – Is the pilot and simulation approach valid?	Pilot plan good, concerned that we have too many parameters and inputs	A	Want to see more customers testing at this stage	N
6	*Pilot results* – Do the results of the pilot support the improvement targets set out in the goal statement?	Pilot results good, minor issues only	G	Has customer testing been adequate?	Y
7	*Learning* – Has the design incorporated key learnings from the pilot?	Yes it has, key links and comment fields have been modified	G	Good	Y
8	*Preferred design* – Will the preferred design deliver the improvement targets set out in the goal statement?	Believe it will, some concerns over uptake and rapid aging of content	A	Agree with concerns, look at the resource required to retain a maintenance team?	N
9	*Customer impact* – Is the impact on Customers of the new process design understood and feasible?	Customer impact understood, more comfortable with the additional customer testing	G	Agree, have we done enough?	Y

Figure 7.1 Design Checklist in DFSS

10	*Supplier impact* – Is the impact on the suppliers of the new process design understood and feasible?	Supplier impact minimal – mostly informational	G	Agree, have we spoken to them?	Y
11	*Risk* – Does the implementation plan address potential problem areas with contingency plans?	Contingency plans – drafts look thorough, still to be fully tested out.	A	Testing, how?	N
12	*Business case* – Will the proposed design deliver the business case?	Business case didn't call for an ongoing help-site maintenance team, costing will have impact on payback but not on overall go-no go decision	G	Agree on final impact; however, "maintenance team" need s to be looked at	Y
13	*Updated project plan* – Is the plan for the Implementation phase robust?	Plan looks good at this stage	G	Agree concerns over any further slippage	Y
14	*Concerns* – Are there any areas of outstanding concern?	Items 5, 8, 11 and 12 above are concerns until we address them	A	Agree; get the team together for a special review ASAP	Y

MBB approvals	Date submitted	Date approved	MBB comments	S
Key outputs – Has the project team delivered the required outputs for the Design phase?	13-Mar-01	18-Mar-01	All key outputs delivered	G
Finance Approval	Date submitted	Date approved	Finance comments	S
Finance approval – Does Finance support the financial business case for this project?	14-Mar-01	18-Mar-01	Valid, should proceed	G
Conclusion	Date submitted	Date approved	Sponsor comments	S
Ongoing validity – Is this still a valid project and should it proceed?	18-Mar-01	23-Mar-01	Valid, should proceed	G

sign-off from a Master Black Belt, Finance and the project sponsor. Since DFSS projects are generally more difficult we recommend that they should only be undertaken by Black Belts that have already completed a DMAIC project successfully.

DFSS Summary

DFSS is a challenging methodology and not for the faint hearted. As we have said before, it is required where incremental improvement is not enough or where there are no existing processes. It is impossible to do justice to the whole DFSS method in one chapter, so be prepared for the SMART things to know about DFSS book!

"If I have seen further it is by standing on the shoulders of giants."

Isaac Newton

"I hear and I forget. I see and I remember. I do and I understand." Confucius

SMART QUOTES

Final Thoughts on Your Six Sigma Success

One final thought before concluding this book. Whether it is DMAIC or DFSS, Six Sigma is not a personality-driven solution. There have been enough failures already where one person or group has claimed the moral high ground on change methodology. Six Sigma is the pulling together of the many different types of tools, techniques and thinking of many "small, medium and large giants". It is an approach that you and your company can use. Good luck, enjoy the experience. Remember there are a lot of people out there who want you to be successful!

Appendix 1

Six Sigma Methods

Affinity Diagrams

Concepts

Affinity diagrams are used to take large amounts of data and to sort them into logical groupings. Most people cannot make use of large numbers of ideas/issues. Affinity diagrams help to simplify ideas and issues into simpler groupings. When a project team needs to simplify a large number of ideas or issues into groups, the use of affinity diagram analysis:

• provides a logical and structured approach to analysing issues; and

• enables new insights and conclusions.

Affinity diagrams must be complete and show all options. Participants undertake a process of brainstorming, presenting and clustering the ideas and agreeing groupings.

Methodology

To construct an affinity diagram:

1. Identify the main affinity diagram topic.

2. Give each participant a fixed number of post-it notes (e.g. 5-10).

3. Brainstorm issues and allow each individual to fill out their ideas on post-it notes.

4. Ask each participant in turn to present noe post-it note idea.

5. Group similar ideas by putting the post-it notes next to each other.

6. Continue placing post-it notes until all ideas have been presented.

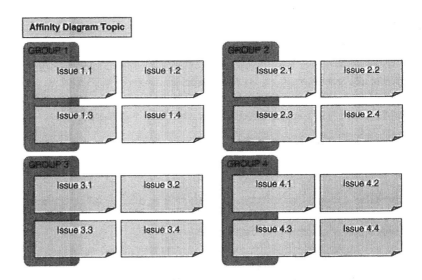

Figure A1 Affinity diagram example format.

7. Work with the group to confirm clusters and to name each cluster.

8. Put the name of each cluster on a different coloured post-it note to show that it is a heading.

9. Agree conclusions and next steps.

Affinity diagrams require participants to have the background information on the issues to be analysed. Participants should include the project team and those who have a detailed knowledge of the main issues. It works best with groups of between five and eight people.

Figure A1 shows as example affinity diagram.

Affinity diagram good practices

- Silent brainstorming is effective in allowing all people to have an equal say.

- Affinity diagrams can be combined with brainstorming sessions.

- Different coloured post-it notes can be used to show different topic areas.

Critical to quality (CTQ) analysis

Concepts

Critical to quality analysis is designed to give a project team good insight into the real needs of a customer. It consists of two elements: the 'voice of the customer' (VoC); and CTQ measures.

Customer needs are at the core of any integrated Six Sigma or quality process. When a project team needs a detailed understanding of customer needs, CTQ analysis:

• provides a logical and structured approach to analysing issues; and

• enables new insights and conclusions.

CTQ analysis must be complete in showing all options. The process involves identifying the VoC and then establishing CTQ measures.

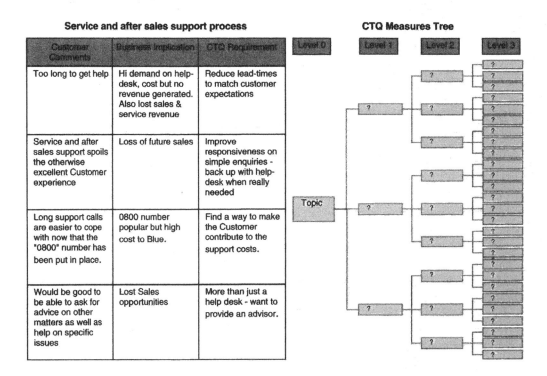

Figure A2 *CTQ analysis example.*

Methodology

1. Identify the customer process to be analysed.

2. List the main comments made by customers about this process.

3. List the business implications of each customer comment.

4. List the CTQ customer requirements.

5. Identify Level 0 and Level 1 CTQ measures.

6. Expand CTQ measures to Level 2 and Level 3 as required.

7. Agree the conclusions and next steps.

8. Enter VoC analysis and CTQ measures into DMAIC tool.

CTQ analysis requires participants to have the relevant information to hand. This is likely to include customer surveys, complaints data, sales reports and returns reports. Participants should include the project team and people who have a detailed knowledge of the customer process.

Figure A2 shows an example CTQ analysis.

CTQ analysis good practices

• Talk to customers and suppliers about their needs.

• Talk to customer service, delivery and returns staff.

• Focus on substantive data rather than perceptions about what customers require.

"Day-in-the-life" study

Concepts

A "day-in-the-life" study is used to analyse current jobs for non-value-added activities, and describe the future activities of a job when planned changes have been implemented.

A "day-in-the-life" study works on the following principles:

- Not all work activities contribute to the achievement of business objectives.

- It is difficult to see value-added and non-value-added activities in somebody else's job.

- Systematic analysis of job activities can help to explain value.

- The value of new jobs can be explained using "day-in-the-life" scenarios.

Methodology

1. Identify the job or role to be reviewed.

2. Confirm the brief job description and overall purpose for the role.

3. List the key five performance objectives for the role.

4. On a regular basis throughout the day list the activities performed and timing.

5. At the end of the day assess how much each contributed towards objectives.

6. Make comments where there are concerns or where activities could be changed.

	ROLE DEFINITION			PERFORMANCE OBJECTIVES
Job title or role	Senior Account Manager		O1	Maximise profitable sales
Role description	Managing sales and customer relationships		O2	Increase positive market brand awareness
Role purpose	To maximise sales from target accounts		O3	Communicate market and competitor trends internally
Date of analysis	23rd November 200+		O4	Contribute to new product development
RAG summary	Red = 24%, Amber = 45%, Green = 31%		O5	

TIME	ACTIVITY	O1	O2	O3	O4	O5	COMMENTS	
8.30am	Open and respond to emails	I	I					
8.45am	Prepare for internal project meeting				I			
9.02am	Attend project meeting on client implementation				I		Involvement in project meetings is of questionable value so long as the hand-over brief works - do differently!	A
10.25am	Discuss account problems with technical team	D	I					
11.00am	Meet with marketing resource to plan campaign	I	D				No clear meeting objectives or agenda set - lots of wasted time and no clear action items	A
12.30pm	Meet Sales Director for lunch	I		I	I			
1.25pm	Travel to client						Potential to issue account managers with mobile phones	
2.30pm	Initial client briefing	D	I					
2.35pm	Presentation to client team	D	D				Better preparation and planning would have allowed questions to be resolved - use a generic pack	
2.55pm	Return to head office						Potential to issue account managers with mobile phones	
3.45pm	Write up notes on meeting and arrange follow up actions	D						
4.00pm	Updated expenses on the new intranet						This activity is duplicated using paper and technology	
4.10pm	Make customer calls to set up meetings and clarify issues	D	I					
4.30pm	Write a brief internal briefing document based on Win-Loss			D	D		Standardise the template for recording win-loss will make it easier for others to retrieve and re-use	A
5.15pm	Update forecasts and CRM system						Large amount of bureaucracy and takes too long - a new system might speed this up and reduce frustration	A
6.00pm	Close system and go home							

Figure A3 A "day in the life" study example.

7. Assess the overall status for each activity assigning it as red, amber or green, where:

    Red: indicates non-value-added activity and should be eliminated;

    Amber: indicates inefficient use of time and method should be changed;

    Green: indiates activity that contributes directly to objectives in an efficient manner.

8. Summarize the percentage of time in each category (red, amber, green).

A "day in the life" study requires participants to have a formal job description and performance expectations for the role of interest. Participants should include the project team and people who's jobs will be impacted by planned changes.

Figure A3 shows an example of a "day-in-the-life" study.

Good Practices

- People often resist any analysis of how they spend their time, make it easy to contribute.

- Focus on the non-value-added activities that people want to eliminate.

- Ensure data is typical, not an unusual day.

Decision analysis

Concepts

The decision analysis tool provides a systematic approach to decision making. The tool is designed to help project teams make good decisions and to understand why some decisions may be better than other.

Decision analysis works on the following principles:

- The best decision makers use a balance of creative and rational techniques.

- Involve others to increase commitment to the decision.

- Selection criteria should be balanced in terms of time, cost and performance measures.

- Understanding business concerns helps to focus on the critical decisions.

- Creatively combining alternatives often provides the best solution overall.

Methodology

1. Identify critical business decisions and ensure that the right people are involved.

2. Understand the business concerns (or problem).

3. Identify alternative solutions and boil the list down to the top four.

4. Confirm that each solution is well understood by all in the group

5. Quickly screen options against four generic criteria: SAFE
   S   Is it SUITABLE given the current situation or strategy?
   A   Is it ACCEPTABLE to all key stakeholders involved?
   F   Is it FEASIBLE given time and resource constraints?
   E   Will it ENDURE beyond the immediate short-term period?

6. Identify the criteria that will be used to make the decision.

7. Assess the relative weight of each criteria – most important one scores 10.

8 Score each alternative option against the criteria using a 10-point scale.

9. Use the weighted score to make the final choice - consider combining options.

10. Ensure the group have bought into the solution and that concerns are resolved.

					S	A	F	E
1. DECISION PURPOSE								
To recommend a replacement wash and paint station for line two cabinets								
2. BUSINESS CONCERNS				**IMPACT ON PERFORMANCE**				
The current machine leaks and needs cleaning fluid replacement at twice the rate of machines on line one				5% down-time on day shift and 25% cleaning fluid cost over-run				
3. OPTIONS		**KEY FEATURES**			S	A	F	E
A	EuroPharma - model KL70	Split tank, 100 litre / min, 1000 capacity, 10 minute recycle - £75,000			G	G	G	G
B	Siemens XKX 250	Split tank, 250 litre, 1500 capacity, 15 minute recycle - £125,000			G	A	G	G
C	Techno - 2000	Triple tank, auto circulating, total 3,000 litre - zero downtime - £175,000			G	G	A	G
D	Constores - mid series	Part owned by major competitor			G	R	G	R
4. SELECTION CRITERIA		**IDEAL PERFORMANCE**	A	A	B	C	D	WtA	WtB	WtC	WtD
1	Minimise operating downtime	No downtime during tank change	8	7	5	10		49	35	70	0
2	Minimise purchase cost	No adverse impact on annual operating budget	6	10	7	5		100	70	50	0
3	Minimise maintenance costs and complexity	Option of alternative spares supply	7	4	10	7		16	40	28	0
4	Maximise cabinet clean quality	Zero rejects due to poor cleaning	10	5	10	8		25	50	40	0
5	Maximise consistency with other lines / spares	Consistency of supplies and	3	10	9	5		100	90	50	0
6	Minimise time to implementation	Ability to install over the summer shut down	7	5	10	4		25	50	20	0
7	Minimise training requirements	Uses same control process as current machine	4	10	8	4		100	80	40	0
							Totals	415	415	298	0
5. FINAL DECISION								
Siemens XKX 250 with reconfigured change over process to increase downtime performance								

Figure A4 *Decision analysis example.*

Decision analysis requires participants to have detailed information on the major options being considered. Participants should include those with relevant expertise and creative ideas as well as those who can help with sponsorship and buy-in.

Figure A4 shows an example of decision analyis.

Good practices

- Don't jump to the first solution that is presented.

- You need enough people to understand the decision options.

- Too many people will slow down the process.

- Not involving the right people will result in lack of buy-in to the decision.

Forcefield analysis

Concepts

Forcefield analysis is a visual tool for helping with problem solving, reducing resistance and implementing change. It shows the type and strength of forces that will drive and resist change.

Forcefield analysis works on the following principles:

- Not everyone accepts and supports proposed changes.

- Supporting (or driving) forces can be used to drive positive change through.

- Opposing (or resisting) forces must be recognised and overcome.

- Change should not start until the balance is positive.

Methodology

1. Identify the issue

2. Brainstorm the driving forces – factors that strongly support the planned changes.

3. Then brainstorm the restraining forces – factors that act as obstacles to change.

4. Then assess the relative impact or strength of each force.

5. Look at the overall balance and check whether the change should continue.

6. List actions to exploit the supporting forces.

7. List actions to address the resisting forces.

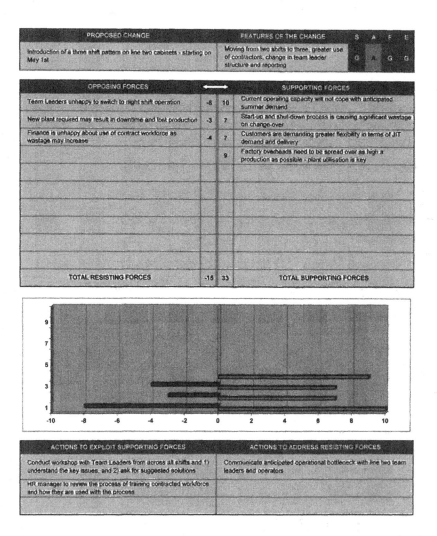

PROPOSED CHANGE	FEATURES OF THE CHANGE	S	A	F	E
Introduction of a three shift pattern on line two cabinets - starting on May 1st	Moving from two shifts to three, greater use of contractors, change in team leader structure and reporting	G	A	G	G

OPPOSING FORCES			SUPPORTING FORCES
Team Leaders unhappy to switch to night shift operation	-6	10	Current operating capacity will not cope with anticipated summer demand
New plant required may result in downtime and lost production	-3	7	Start-up and shut-down process is causing significant wastage on change-over
Finance is unhappy about use of contract workforce as wastage may increase	-4	7	Customers are demanding greater flexibility in terms of JIT demand and delivery
		9	Factory overheads need to be spread over as high a production as possible - plant utilisation is key
TOTAL RESISTING FORCES	-15	33	TOTAL SUPPORTING FORCES

ACTIONS TO EXPLOIT SUPPORTING FORCES	ACTIONS TO ADDRESS RESISTING FORCES
Conduct workshop with Team Leaders from across all shifts and 1) understand the key issues, and 2) ask for suggested solutions	Communicate anticipated operational bottleneck with line two team leaders and operators
HR manager to review the process of training contracted workforce and how they are used with the process	

Figure A5 Forcefield analysis example.

8. Agree next steps.

Forcefield analysis requires participants to have detailed information on the major options being considered. Participants should include those with relevant expertise and creative ideas as well as those who can help with sponsorship and buy-in.

Figure A5 shows an example of forcefield analysis.

Good practices

- Involving people helps to build trust and improve understanding/buy-in.

- Make sure planned changes will have sufficient resources allocated to them to help them to succeed.

Issue trees

Concepts

Issue tree diagrams (a.k.a. structure tree diagrams) show the linkages between issues and provide a structure of levels for thinking about issues and ideas. They are commonly used when a project team needs to understand and simplify complex issues and their linkages.

Issue trees:

- provide a logical and structured approach to analysing issues;

- enable new insights and conclusions;

- must be complete, showing all options.

Methodology

1. Identify the main issue tree issue (level 0).

2. Define the need for change from the current position.

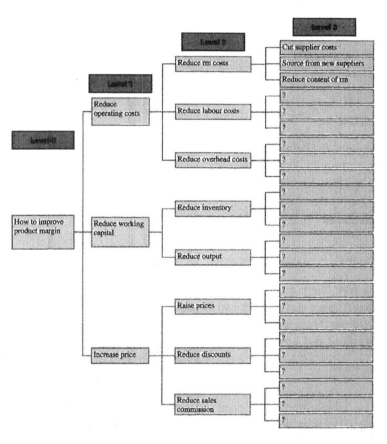

Figure A6 Issue tree analysis example.

3. Identify the next level of issues in the tree (level 1).

4. Work through the Level 1 issues to create the level 2 issues.

5. Continue to work through the next level of issues (level 3 and beyond) to develop conclusions.

6. Agree the conclusions and next steps.

Issue tree analysis requires participants to have background information on the issues being analysed. Participants should include the project team and those who have a detailed knowledge of the main issues.

Figure A6 shows an example of an issue tree analysis.

Good practices

• A yes/no structure to issues can help to force out insights.

• Issue trees can be combined with yes/no options to be decision trees.

• Each issue tree should be complete in its coverage of a topic.

Moments-of-truth (MoT) analysis

Concepts

Moments-of-truth are points in the process, time or interactions when customers will form a view about the quality of a product or service. MoT analysis helps a project team to see clearly where the critical points of customer interaction take place in a process.

MoT analysis works on the following principles:

- Customers are the most important stakeholder for any commercial business.

- All customer interactions will impact on the customer's perceptions.

- Everyone in the business should understand who their customers are.

- All interactions should be identified and proactively managed.

- Service-level expectations should be set in conjunction with the customer.

Methodology

1. Identify the process to be reviewed and agree its scope and boundaries.

2. List out all of the major activities in the process.

3. Identify all critical points of customer interaction – moments-of-truth.

4. For each MoT, specify who internally is responsible.

5. Agree the appropriate service level for each MoT.

6. Confirm current service levels and targets.

7. Contrast current performance against service level targets.

8. Use red–amber–green to identify the current status of each MoT.

9. Identify improvement opportunities and next steps.

MoT analysis requires participants to have background information on the processes being analysed such as customer process maps, complaints data, service levels, etc. Participants should include the project team and those who are close to customers/customer interactions.

CUSTOMER MoT	SERVICE LEVEL	PERFORMANCE	OWNER	RAG	IMPROVEMENT ACTIONS
Key activities within this process	Customer agreed service levels	Current performance against service levels	Person responsible for performance for each MoT		Future actions to improve the performance level in each MoT
Customer places order for cabinets	100% online acceptance of order	System sharing resulting in 80% instant access	John Mactear	A	Removing sharing of system with line B so as to increase online access to desired 100% level
Customer receives update on delivery and fulfillment	100% instant confirmation	Instant if online, otherwise 5 mins	Sally Claessens	G	
Customer submits a change request	Ability to change order timing up to 30mins pre-delivery	Orders changed up to 10mins pre-delivery	John Mactear	G	
Customer receives cabinet	100% received within 4hr of order	80% due to supplier stockouts	Sally Claessens	A	Reviewing service level agreement with supplier, and second sourcing

Figure A7 Moments-of-truth example.

Figure A7 shows an example MoT analysis.

Good Practices

- Don't assume you understand customer needs – go and ask them.

- Don't expect all customers to want the same things – look for natural segments.

- Look at the data from the customers' perspective.

Process maps

Concepts

Process maps show the key stages of a process and the linkages between activities. They can be enhanced by adding in detail on volumes and values. They are commonly used to aid understanding and analysis of business workflows, and to identify opportunities for improvement.

Process mapping works on the following principles:

- All repeatable activities take place within "business processes".

- For every activity there will typically be an input and an output.

- The customer is the most important player in any process.

- Processes should be as simple as possible with a minimum of hand-overs between groups.

- Processes should be managed and regularly reviewed.

Methodology

1. Clearly identify the process to be reviewed and define the boundaries.

2. Ensure the right people are involved in developing the process map.

3. Identify the "role players" – the different groups of people involved in the process.

4. Brainstorm the various activities occurring throughout the process.

5. Put them into the right order and assign each to one primary group.

6. Draw the interconnections between the activities.

7. Add in data on the volume and value of process flows (where possible).

8. Identify all decision points where the process may go in several directions.

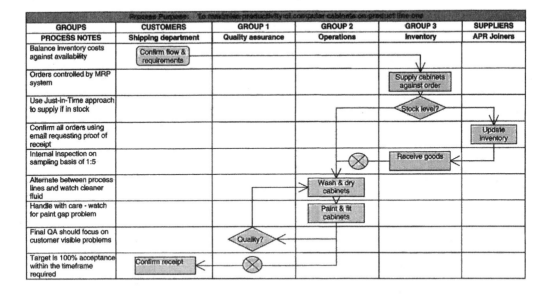

Figure A8 Process map example.

9. Identify the natural points for monitoring and controlling the process.

10. Reflect back on the process and look for opportunities to simplify it.

11. Review the process with customers and supplier to check it is correct.

Process mapping requires participants to have background information on the processes being analysed. Participants should include the project team and those who have a detailed knowledge of the process. Customers and suppliers can also be involved.

Figure A8 shows an example of a process map.

Good practices

- First agree on the process purpose, scope and objectives – then map it.

- Always use an activity-versus-role map so that handovers are clearly identified.

- Create a simple outline first, then go into detail.

SIPOC

Concepts

SIPOC stands for Supplier–Inputs–Process–Outputs–Customer. It is a high-level process flow that gives a project team an overview of the process being analysed and improved. A SIPOC analysis is designed to assist understanding of the critical stages of a process and how it impacts customers and suppliers.

SIPOC works on the following principles:

- SIPOC diagrams are used to scope the work of a process improvement team.

- It is often used in combination with the process map tool.

- This analysis helps to identify key process stakeholders.

- SIPOC diagrams also help to define the boundaries of a process and project scope.

Methodology

1. Ensure the right people are involved in the group analysis.

2. Identify the process and boundaries.

3. State the primary purpose of the process.

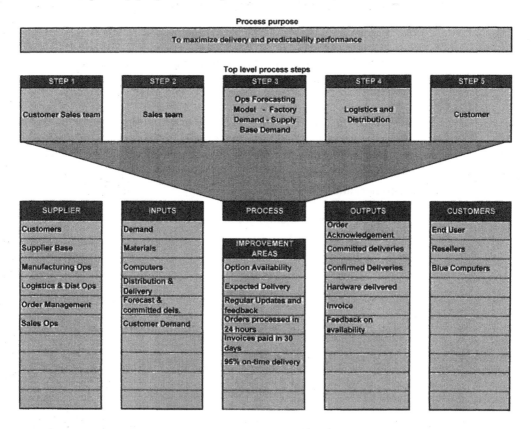

Figure A9 SIPOC example.

4. Start with the process map – keep it to four or five high-level steps.

5. Identify the outputs of this process.

6. List the customers that will receive the outputs.

7. Identify the inputs that the process requires.

8. List the suppliers of inputs to the process.

9. Identify key areas where improvements are required.

10. Agree areas for further analysis and next steps.

SIPOC requires participants to have background information on the processes being analysed including existing process maps, quality manuals, and customer and supplier lists. Participants should include the project team and those who have a detailed knowledge of the processes, customers and suppliers.

Figure A9 shows an example of SIPOC analysis

Good practices

• Create a process map if more detailed interactions need to be shown.

• Get the whole team involved in the SIPOC at an early stage.

• Look for Moments of Truth (MoT) with customers.

• Remember to keep the SIPOC at a high level.

• Be clear about the boundaries of the process (e.g. where the project scope starts and ends).

SWOT analysis

Concepts

SWOT is a structured approach to identify the internal and external forces that drive an organization's competitive position. It considers *strengths*, *weaknesses*, *opportunities* and *threats*.

SWOT analysis is used to identify the key areas of impact so that plans can be made to improve the competitive position of the business by addressing the most appropriate area.

A SWOT should be used when the project team needs more understanding of the external environment and internal capabilities

- Internal analysis focuses on strengths and weaknesses of current capabilities.

- External analysis focuses on opportunities and threats in the market.

- The SWOT analysis should be balanced across all four areas.

- Priorities ideas within an area.

- Use the SWOT analysis to create insights and action.

Methodology

1. Clearly state the topic for the SWOT analysis – what is in and what is out.

2. Agree a time limit for the analysis.

3. Assign a facilitator and a time keeper.

4. Analyse the *internal environment* by brainstorming strengths and weaknesses:

Strengths any potential resource or capability that provides a competitive advantage;

Weaknesses any existing/potential force which could inhibit a competitive advantage.

5. Analyse the *external environment* by brainstorming opportunities and threats:

Opportunities any existing/potential force that could provide competitive advantage;

Threats any existing/potential force that could inhibit a competitive advantage.

6. Clarify ideas group review. Have any questions clarified by the person who gave the idea.

7. Narrow the list by giving each idea a score of up to 10 for the ones with the highest impact

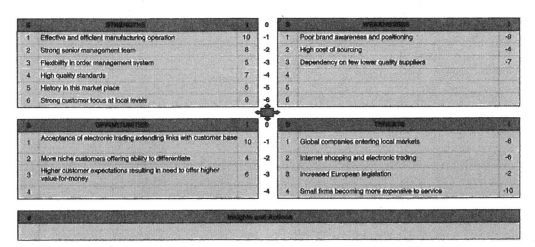

Figure A10 SWOT example.

8. Agree the most significant areas to focus on.

9. Identify the key insights and the actions required.

SWOT requires participants to have existing data on the internal and external competitive environment. Participants should include those with real insights into the issues.

Figure A10 shows an example of SWOT analysis.

Good practices

• Pay equal attention to each area – don't just focus on one or two.

• Keep a good balance of external and internal issues.

• Limit comments to a maximum of 10 per area.

• Don't just take the first quick answers – explore possibilities.

Fishbone diagram

Concepts

This is a visual analytical tool (sometimes called a Ishikawa or cause-and-effect diagram) that displays the grouped causes (fish bones) that contribute to a problem (the head of the fish). It is a systematic method for exploring cause and effect relationships in order to establish the root cause of a problem. The fishbone tool is very useful for illustrating the combination of contributing factors. Most Six Sigma projects will require the project team to produce a root cause analysis.

Methodology

1. Set up a group meeting.

2. Write down the effect being investigated on the right-hand side of the fishbone diagram.

3. Write down the four major categories relevant to the effect spaced out over the diagram. Categories could be from the list below or adapted to the situation:
   4Ms   manpower, methods, materials, machinery
   4Ps   people, processes, policies, place/plant
   4Ss   surroundings, suppliers, systems, skills

4. Breakdown the causes in each category through brainstorming. Write them on the lines of the diagram.

5. Continue to ask the question "What else?" until there are no more answers.

6. Discuss each category and cause in turn and identify the most probable causes (MPC). Mark them on the chart

7. Agree an action plan to investigate the most probable causes – what, who, when.

Fishbone diagram analysis requires participants to have information about the effect and initial ideas on possible causes. Participants should include the project team and those who have expertise in the problem area.

Figure A11 shows an example of a fishbone diagram.

Good practices

• Use the five whys – see Glossary.

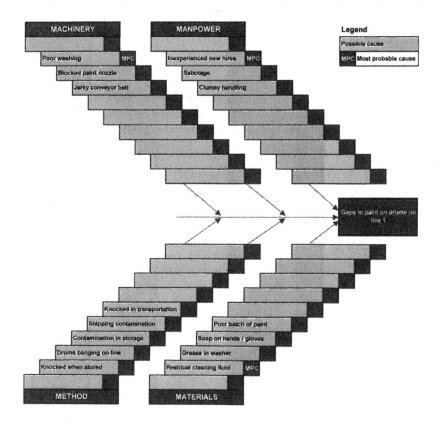

Figure A11 Fishbone diagram example.

- Use brainstorming (see below).
- Constantly focus attention on what is major or a minor cause and why.

Brainstorming

Concepts

Brainstorming is a method for helping a group of people to develop a list of ideas about a specific topic. The objective is to generate large numbers of ideas quickly and efficiently. Brainstorming can be useful at many stages of a project but it is good to brainstorm early!

Brainstorming works on the following principles:

- Brainstorming is about generating a large number and wide breadth of ideas.

- The group should avoid criticizing ideas – evaluation comes later,

- Encourage free-wheeling (i.e. open thinking),

Methodology

1. Set up a meeting for a group of 5–10 people.

2. Nominate a facilitator (a neutral role).

3. Set the topic (issue/opportunity).

4. Agree guidelines with the group (e.g. don't evaluate).

5. Brainstorm ideas use flipchart or post-it notes.

6. Encourage contributions from all the people present.

7. Create groupings for the ideas.

8. Agree which ideas are valid for this project.

9. Prioritize the ideas.

10. Agree next steps and responsibilities.

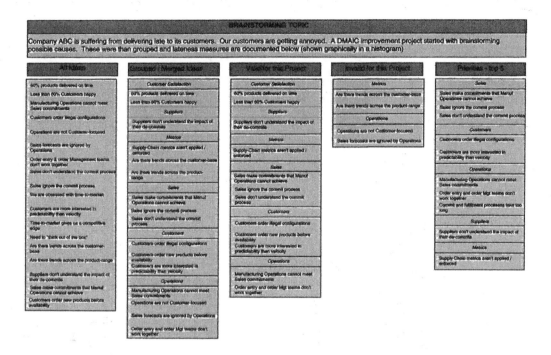

Figure A12 Brainstorming example.

Brainstorming requires participants to have existing data, and an open mind to think "out of the box". Participants should include those with good ideas and insights on the topic.

Figure A12 gives an example of brainstorming.

Good practices

- People should have knowledge of the topic/process being brainstormed.

- The facilitator should be neutral and careful not to take a position.

- Encourage contributions from everyone – don't allow a few to dominate.

- Ask "what if?".

Appendix 2

Six Sigma Statistics

Histogram

Concepts

A histogram is a bar chart where each bar represents the frequency one of a distinct range of possible outcomes, causes or events. A histogram is a way of graphically representing the relative frequency of outcomes. It facilitates visual analysis of the distribution of outcomes (central value, range and shape of distributions), enabling the observer to draw initial conclusions about the process or population.

A histogram is constructed by repeating the process and recording the outcome for each repetition. The analyst must define an appropriate set of "buckets", each representing one of the distinct possible outcomes. Buckets may be a discrete value or a defined range of values. Outcomes score a "count" against the relevant bucket each time the process is repeated. The number of repartitions may be arbitrarily decided or defined by a prescribed time frame. Ideally, a histogram will incorporate at least 50 data points (outcomes).

Interpretation of a histogram

1. Bell curve – symmetrical (normal distribution). The most frequently occurring event is central in the distribution with the remainder evenly distributed on either side.

2. Jagged sawtooth pattern – no real pattern exists; the measurement system may be flawed.

3. Skewed to one side – this pattern is common when measuring counting or time problems. A long-tailed distribution may indicate that the data comes from a process that is not easily explained by simple statistical techniques.

4. Two or more peaks – this could indicate that there is more than one factor influencing the outcome.

5. Flat data pattern – this distribution would indicate that all outcomes are equally likely.

6. Dominant value(s) – this pattern indicates that certain event(s) are significantly more likely to occur than others in the range of possible events.

Histogram example

Problem/opportunity definition
A company wants to determine the average call time and the distribution of call duration in its customer care call centre. Management has defined a number of equal call duration ranges. (Note: No call lasted longer than 15 minutes.)

Data and results

Buckets	Total
0–3	180
>3–6	1,209
>6–9	3,408
>9–12	1,133
>12–15	175

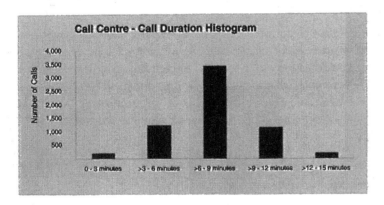

Figure A13

The histogram (Figure A13) shows that the majority of call centre calls last between 6 and 9 minutes. As there is a sequential relationship between the possible outcomes (i.e. time line), we can also observe that call durations appear to be normally distributed about the average (Result 1: bell curve). A detailed analysis using more sophisticated statistical tools would enable determination of the mean and standard deviation of the distribution of call durations.

Pareto chart

Concepts

Pareto charts are used to graphically represent the relative impact of events (sales of different products, defect types, etc.) on some predetermined outcome (profitability, total number of defects, etc.). They are often used to assist in identifying the most appropriate starting position for a project.

A Pareto chart is constructed by collecting the data that quantifies the impact of each event on the outcome of interest. The events are then arranged in tabular form in order of highest impact to lowest (*x*-axis). If using a percentage chart, calculate the percentage of total value of each of the events and arrange them in order of decreasing value (*x*-axis). The *y*-axis represents either the range of values or the range 0–100% or both.

Interpretation of a Pareto chart

1. Curve starting steeply near origin then tapering/flattening out, tall bars starting near the origin then decreasing rapidly in height with a long tail of short bars: These patterns indicate that a small percentage of events are responsible for the majority of the total impact on the outcome. The bar heights clearly show the relative impact of all events.

2. Straight line increasing at steady even rate from origin, bars decreasing in height gradually along the *x*-axis: These patterns indicate that the total impact on the outcome is fairly evenly distributed across all events.

Pareto example

Problem/Opportunity Definition

A computer manufacturer uses a quality control system to ensure all product is defect free prior to despatch. All defects are recorded along with the cause or type. Over a period of six months the number of computers found to have defects was 2,620 out of a total of 30,130 produced. Management is embarking on an improvement programme to try to reduce the amount of rework required. A Pareto analysis has been selected to assist management to focus on the area with the highest level of opportunity for improvement.

Data and results

Defect type	Number	Percentage	Cumulative %
Cabinet surface flaw	1,103	42	42
Screen surface flaw	878	34	76
Keyboard not working properly	222	8	84
Mouse not working properly	186	7	91
A-drive not working correctly	97	4	95
D-drive not working	52	2	97
Screen flickers or poor picture quality	32	1	98
USB port not responding correctly	24	1	99
Sound not travelling through speakers correctly	19	1	100
Substandard sound quality through headphones	7	0	100

Interpretation

The Pareto chart (Figure A14) clearly indicates that the two vital areas

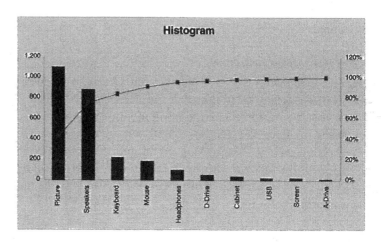

Histogram

Figure A14

requiring attention are picture quality and speaker quality. These two defect types currently account for 76% of all defectives and therefore offer the greatest improvement opportunity.

Run chart

Concepts

A run chart explores the relationships between events and time. It uses a line graph with events plotted along a time-line and a horizontal median line. A "run" is a series of points on the same side of the median line. Points lying on the median line are ignored. Run charts are an effective way of graphically representing variation in a process over time. They help in tracking useful information for predicting trends and cycles and analysing the impact of changes on the process.

A run chart is constructed by observing events at regular intervals over a defined period of time and recording these along the appropriate time-line. The median of all outcomes is calculated and the horizontal "median line" (middle value when events are sorted in order of value rather than time sequence) is also plotted onto the chart. Runs are observed above and below the median line.

Interpretation of a run chart

1. The number of runs you expect to see for a "stable" process depends on the number of data points observed. "Runs test" upper and lower limits can be found in run chart tables.

2. Too many runs may indicate that there is a problem with the process or that something in the process has changed. If short runs (one or two data points) alternate above and below the median line, it may suggest a relationship between process outcomes.

3. Too few runs may indicate a problem with the process or that something in the process has changed. It could also be attributed to a normal cycle in operations. The latter can be checked by conducting a "runs test" for the same period in earlier years.

4. Six or more points in a run continuously increasing or decreasing may indicate a trend.

5. Eight or more points in a run may indicate a shift or major change in the process.

Run chart example

Problem/opportunity definition
A manufacturing company wanted to test the variability in the number of defects in one of its production runs over the period of a day. Man-

agement specifically wanted to know if there were particular times in the day when they should focus their attention.

Data and results

Defects	Time	Defects	Time	Defects	Time	Defects	Time
12	18:30	9	12:30	11	06:30	12	00:30
10	19:00	11	13:00	12	07:00	18	01:00
14	19:30	14	13:30	18	07:30	14	01:30
15	20:00	17	14:00	14	08:00	12	02:00
13	20:30	16	14:30	16	08:30	11	02:30
14	21:00	15	15:00	14	09:00	12	03:00
11	21:30	12	15:30	17	09:30	15	03:30
11	22:00	13	16:00	12	10:00	15	04:00
16	22:30	14	16:30	10	10:30	9	04:30
9	23:00	15	17:00	11	11:00	13	05:00

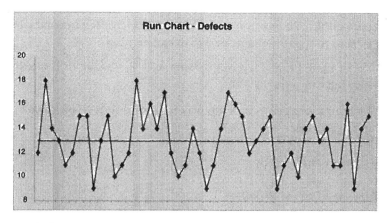

Figure A15

| 14 | 23:30 | 9 | 17:30 | 14 | 11:30 | 15 | 05:30 |
| 15 | 24:00 | 11 | 18:00 | 12 | 12:00 | 10 | 06:00 |

Interpretation

Number of runs = 20   Median value = 13
Lower run limit = 17   Upper run limit = 28

We can see (Figure A15) that the number of runs falls between the upper and lower limits given,[1] indicating that there is a "standard" amount of variability in the number of defects occurring in the process being tested. There are no particularly long runs, the longest being five data points, indicating that there is no time of the day that stands out as being more susceptible to defects than other times of the day.

Control chart

Concepts

A control chart plots time-ordered data with a central horizontal line at the mean. Two statistically determined "control lines" are also plotted. These represent the limits in the amount of variation in the process that is deemed normal or acceptable. They provide a statistical framework for separating common cause variation from special cause variation thereby helping to focus improvement efforts in the right areas.

A control chart is constructed by observing events at regular intervals over a defined period of time and recording these along the appropriate time-line. The mean of all outcomes and the upper (UCL) and lower (LCL) control limits are calculated using the standard formulas.

[1]Upper and lower limits are given on a run chart table and can be found in most statistical texts.

With n observations, there will be m moving ranges (MR) where $m = n - 1$

$$MR_i = |x_{i+1} - x_i|$$

UCL = the average of all observations + 2.66 × the average of all moving ranges

LCL = the average of all observations − 2.66 × the average of all moving ranges

Interpretation of a control chart

1. If all points on the graph lie between the upper and lower control limits, it is assumed that the process is "in control". The variation over the time period measured is deemed common cause variation and not special cause variation (unless some other signal of special cause is present).

2. Data points that fall outside the upper and lower control limits are considered caused by special cause variation (variation from assignable causes). Further investigation may be required to identify the special causes for these outliers.

Control chart example

Problem/opportunity definition

A manufacturing company wanted to test the variability in the number of defects in one of its production runs over the period of a day. Management specifically wanted to know if there were particular times in the day when they should focus their attention.

Data and results

Defects	Time	Defects	Time	Defects	Time	Defects	Time
12	18:30	9	12:30	11	06:30	12	00:30
10	19:00	11	13:00	12	07:00	18	01:00
14	19:30	14	13:30	18	07:30	14	01:30
15	20:00	17	14:00	14	08:00	12	02:00
13	20:30	16	14:30	16	08:30	11	02:30
14	21:00	15	15:00	14	09:00	12	03:00
11	21:30	12	15:30	17	09:30	15	03:30
11	22:00	13	16:00	12	10:00	15	04:00
16	22:30	14	16:30	10	10:30	9	04:30
9	23:00	15	17:00	11	11:00	13	05:00
14	23:30	9	17:30	14	11:30	15	05:30
15	24:00	11	18:00	12	12:00	10	06:00

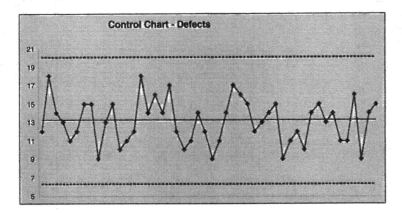

Figure A16

Interpretation

The mean = 13.25   MR-bar = 2.59
UCL = 20.14   LCL = 6.36

All the points on the graph in Figure A16 lie between the upper and lower control limits. We can therefore assume that the variation over the time period measured can be accounted for by common cause variation.

The normal distribution

Concepts

A normal distribution (bell curve: see Figure A17) has its mean in the centre of the distribution. The population mean is μ and the population standard deviation is σ. The notation for this distribution is $X \sim N(\mu{:}\sigma^2)$. This distribution can be converted into the standard normal distribution $Z \sim N(0{:}1)$ using the relationship $Z = (X - \mu)/\sigma$. This is called the Z score of X.

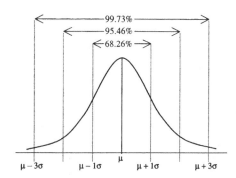

Figure A17

The normal distribution has applications such as setting specifications, making predictions and obtaining probabilities, checking that a process is in control, and deciding the validity of confidence intervals and significance tests. Analyses using the normal distribution require the use of a Z-table or t-tables for sample sizes of less than 30.

Example: finding a probability in a normal distribution

Problem/opportunity definition
A confectionery packaging company would like to know the probability that one of their 1 kg packets of mixed sweets contains 56 or more sweets. The distribution of the number of sweets in a 1 kg packet is $X \sim N(43,36)$.

Calculations and results
$Z = (56 - 43) \div 6 = 2.1667$

From the Z-tables, a Z-score of 2.1667 or more has a probability of 0.0154.

Interpretation
We conclude that the occurrence of a 1 kg packet of sweets containing 56 or more sweets has a probability of 0.015. In other words, 1.5% of the population of 1 kg packets of mixed sweets will contain 56 or more sweets.

Example: finding a confidence interval for a normal distribution

Problem/opportunity definition
A confectionery packaging company would like to know the 95% confidence interval for the number of sweets in their 1 kg packets of mixed

sweets. The distribution of the number of sweets in a 1 kg packet is $X \sim N(43,36)$.

Calculations and results
From the Z-tables, we find the Z-score for a 95% confidence interval ($Z_{\alpha/2}$ where $\alpha = 0.05$) by looking for the corresponding "tail" probability under the curve [i.e. $(1-0.95) \div 2 = 0.025$]. Given that a confidence interval is a two-sided test, the Z-score $= \pm 1.96$.

The 95% confidence interval $= \mu \pm Z \times \sigma = 43 \pm (1.96 \times 6) = \{31.2402 < X < 54.7598\}$.

Interpretation
We conclude that we can be 95% confident that the number of sweets in a 1 kg packet is between 31.24 and 54.76. In other words, 95% of 1 kg packets of mixed sweets will contain between 31.24 and 54.76 sweets.

Simple linear regression (SLR)

Concepts
Simple linear regression quantifies the relationship between an independent variable (x) and a dependent variable (y) for the purposes of explanation and prediction.

The simple linear regression model is: $Y = \beta_0 + \beta_1 x + \varepsilon$ where β_0 is the intercept and β_1 is the slope (change in y per unit increase in x). It is estimated by: $y = b_0 + b_1 x$.

The method used to generate the regression equation is called the method of least squares. It uses the squares of the residuals and gives a point estimate of the value of y for a given value of x. The residual (e_i) is the difference between the observed value (Y_i) and the corresponding fitted value (y_i): $e_i = Y_i - y_i$. Analyses of residuals and of the regression coefficients can be conducted to determine the adequacy of the model.

The data is represented graphically on a scatter plot and the regression equation (line of best fit or line of least squares) is plotted over the scatter of observed points.

The sample correlation coefficient (r) is a statistic that describes the strength of the linear relationship between two variables. $r = -1$ indicates perfect negative correlation, while $r = +1$ indicates perfect positive correlation.

If r is close to zero you may wish to test the hypothesis H_0: $\rho = 0$ versus H_1: $\rho \neq 0$, i.e. the hypothesis that the correlation coefficient is equal to zero. (Note: for this hypothesis r is written ρ.)

The null hypothesis is rejected if $|t_0| > t_{\alpha,n-2}$ using a double-sided t-table test. This test assumes that x and y are jointly normally distributed.

The coefficient of determination (R^2) is the square of the correlation coefficient. Expressed as a percentage, it measures the amount of variation in y that can be explained by x.

If the null hypothesis is accepted there is no correlation between x and y.

If the null hypothesis is rejected there is correlation between x and y.

R^2 expressed as a percentage is the amount of variability in the data that can be accounted for by the model.

SLR example

Problem/opportunity definition
A factory is manufacturing widgets on a number of machines. Manage-

ment want to know what, if any, the relationship is between the output of widgets and the age of the machine.

Data and results

Age	0.6	0.9	1.0	0.8	1.6	1.4	1.6	0.6	1.6	0.2	0.5	0.7	1.7	0.4	1.3	1.8	1.5	0.1	1.5	1.9
Output	20	17	17	18	14	17	12	22	13	25	20	18	10	18	15	9	14	24	13	10

Figure A18 plots the results graphically.

Regression statistics

Multiple R	0.94366
R^2	0.89049
Adjusted R^2	0.8844
Standard error	1.54078
Observations	20

	Coefficients	Standard error	t-statistic
Intercept	24.4584655	0.757272621	32.2980983
x variable 1	−7.51932308	0.621530083	−12.0980839

Interpretation
$r = -0.94$, indicating a strong negative correlation between machine age and widget output. $R^2 = 0.8863$, indicating that 88.63% of the variation in the data can be accounted for by the model. $b_0 = 24.25$, indicating that the line of best fit (least squares) crosses the y-axis at 24.25. In other words, the model estimates that the average widget output per hour of a new machine is 24.25. $b_1 = -7.51$, indicating that for

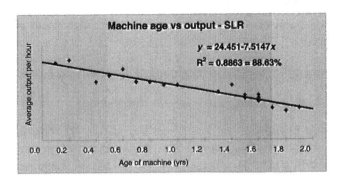

Figure A18

each year a machine is in operation its output will decrease by an average of 7.51 widgets per hour.[2]

Hypothesis testing: independent t-tests and paired t-tests

Concepts

A hypothesis test is a procedure that utilizes statistical formula and tables to draw conclusions about data at a specified level of confidence. Hypothesis testing helps determine whether the variation present is greater than the level of common cause variation expected given the parameters of the distribution.

A hypothesis test can be used to decide many issues including:

[2]Excel and other statistical packages such as MINITAB will create the scatterplot of observed values, calculate the regression coefficients b_0 and b_1, plot the regression equation, find t_0 for testing hypotheses, and calculate the correlation coefficient and the coefficient of determination.

- Do the parameters of a distribution have particular values and relationships?

- Are there differences between groups of data (see tests below)?

- Have there been changes to a specific distribution?

A statistical hypothesis test has a null hypothesis, H_0, describing the value or relationship being tested (e.g. the case that there is no relationship, no difference, no change) and an alternative hypothesis, H_1, describing the alternative case. It has a specified probability value, α, defining the maximum probability that H_0 will be rejected when it is true. The probability that H_0 will be rejected when it is false is called the power of the test, $1 - \beta$.

There are two types of potential error in hypothesis testing: (1) rejecting a null hypothesis that is true, which has a probability of α and is called the P-value; and (2) failing to reject a null hypothesis when it is false, which has a probability of β.

When comparing data from different populations we assume independent, representative (unbiased) samples. When comparing data from different processes we assume stable, representative samples.

A hypothesis test can be either one-tailed or two-tailed.

t-test for independent samples

This is a t-test to compare differences between two independent groups of data. The purpose of the test may be to gauge whether the two samples could be from the same population, or we may wish to know if one is significantly "better" than the other in terms of average output. The hypothesis and formula below test the group averages.

Hypothesis:

H_0: There is no difference between the averages of the two groups.
H_1: There is a difference between the averages of the two groups.

Test value

$$t_0 = \frac{|\bar{x}_1 - \bar{x}_2| - 0}{\sqrt{\dfrac{s_1^2}{n_1} + \dfrac{s_2^2}{n_2}}}$$

where x_1 and x_2 are the averages of group 1 and 2 respectively, s_1 and s_2 are the standard deviations of group 1 and 2 respectively, and n_1 and n_2 are the sample sizes of group 1 and 2 respectively.

Critical value

$t_{\alpha,v}$ where

$$v = \frac{\left[\left(s_1^2 / n_1\right) + \left(s_2^2 / n_2\right)\right]^2}{\left(s_1^2 / n_1\right)^2 + \left(s_2^2 / n_2\right)^2} - 2$$

using double sided t-tables

Interpretation

Reject H_0 if $t_0 >$ the critical value $t_{\alpha,v}$ and conclude that at the $\alpha \times$ 100% significance level, there is a difference between the averages of the two groups. In this case we conclude that the groups are from different populations or that one group average is significantly "better" than the other.

t-test for paired data

This is a test to compare differences between two groups of data where each measure in group 1 has a corresponding measure in group 2. In this case the measures in the two groups are related. They are paired or matched. The purpose of the test may be to gauge whether a change in process has significantly changed output of that process. The difference between each set of paired data is calculated $d_i = x_{i2} - x_{i2}$. To test the difference between the group we use the average of the differences between each data pair, d(bar).

Hypothesis
H_0: $d = 0$ The null hypothesis states that there is no difference between the two groups
H_1: $d \neq 0$

Test value
$$t_0 = \frac{(\bar{d} - 0)\sqrt{n}}{s}$$
where s is the standard deviation of the differences

Critical value
$t_{\alpha,\nu}$ where $\nu = n - 1$.

Interpretation
Reject H_0 if $t_0 >$ the critical value $t_{\alpha,\nu}$ (double-sided t-table) and conclude that at the $\alpha \times 100\%$ significance level, there is a difference between the averages of the two groups.

ANOVA (one-way analysis of variance)

Concepts

One-way analysis of variance uses a completely randomized design to analyse a single factor with two or more levels (or treatments). For a one-way ANOVA, a linear statistical model describes the n observations under each of the k levels:

$$y_{ij} = \mu + \tau_i + \varepsilon_{ij} \text{ for } i = 1 \text{ to } k \text{ and } j = 1 \text{ to } n$$

where y_{ij} is the (ij) observation, μ is the overall mean, τ is the ith level effect, and ε_{ij} is the random error.

ANOVA is used to simultaneously compare multiple group averages.

F-test for differences in group averages

Hypothesis

H_0: $\mu_1 = \mu_2 = \ldots = \mu_k$, i.e. all group averages are equal
H_1: not all μ_i are equal

or equivalently

H_0: $\tau_1 = \tau_2 = \ldots = \tau_k = 0$, i.e. there are no level effects
H_1: not all τ_i equal 0

Test value
F_0 = mean square between groups ÷ mean square within groups (i.e. residual mean square) where the mean square = sum of squares ÷ degrees of freedom

Interpretation
Reject the null hypothesis if $F_0 >$ the critical value $F_{(\alpha, v1, v2)}$ where n_1 is the degrees of freedom of the test value numerator and n_2 is the degrees of freedom of the test value denominator. Conclude that one or more of the group averages is different.

Assumptions

- All samples are from normally distributed populations or processes.

- All samples are representative of the population or process they are from.

- The processes are stable and show no shifts or trends over time. No special cause variation present.

- All group variances are the same. This can also be checked using an *F*-test. See below.

ANOVA example – testing for treatment differences (using Microsoft Excel)

	Type 1	Type 2	Type 3	Type 4	Type 5
Reading 1	54	37	58	37	49
Reading 2	43	54	46	45	52
Reading 3	38	48	58	39	46
Reading 4	48	39	47	38	53
Total	183	178	209	159	200
Average	45.75	44.5	52.25	39.75	50

ANOVA

Source of variation	SS	df	MS	F	P-value	F_{crit}
Between groups	381.7	4	95.425	2.69435	0.07128	3.055575
Within groups	531.25	15	35.4167			
Total	1307.75	19				

Interpretation

$F_{0.05,4,15} = 3.06 > F_0 = 2.69$: therefore we reject the null hypothesis. We conclude that not all treatment averages are equal. At least one of the treatment types yields as average that is significantly different to that of the other treatment types. Further analysis is required to determine which treatment types are significantly different from others.

F-test for differences in group averages

This ANOVA test simultaneously compares multiple group variances.

Hypothesis
H_0: $\sigma_1 = \sigma_2 = ... = \sigma_k$
H_1: not all σ_i are equal

Test value
F_0 = largest group σ ÷ smallest group σ

Interpretation
Reject the null hypothesis if $F_0 >$ the critical value $F_{(\alpha, v1, v2)}$ where v_1 is the degrees of freedom of the designated numerator group, and v_2 is the degrees of freedom of the designated denominator group. Conclude that the group variances are not all equal.

Chi-square test

The chi-square test is used to compare proportions or frequency of occurrences of two or more groups of discrete variables.

To conduct a chi-square test, the observed counts (O_{ij}) and the expected counts (E_{ij}) of each occurrence are recorded in a contingency table. Rows (i) number from 1 to R, and columns (j) number from 1 to C.

E_{ij} = (total of row i × total of column j) ÷ overall total

Hypothesis

H_0: There are no differences between groups.
H_1: Not all groups are equal.

Test value

$$\chi^2_{cal} = \sum_{i=1}^{s} \sum_{j=1}^{t} \frac{\left(E_{ij} - O_{ij}\right)^2}{E_{ij}}$$

Interpretation

Reject the null hypothesis if $\chi^2_{cal} >$ the critical value $\chi^2_{(\alpha,\nu)}$, where $\nu = (R - 1)(C - 1)$.

If the null hypothesis is rejected, the next step is to determine which group proportions are different and why.

Assumptions

• The sample is representative of the population or process.

• The underlying distribution is binomial for discrete data.

• For reliable results, the expected count for each cell must be greater than or equal to 5. If it is not, a larger sample size may be required.

Chi-square test example (using Microsoft Excel)

Problem/opportunity definition

A company wanted to know if there was any difference between the proportion of defects for a number of different treatment types.

Data and results

Observed frequencies
Column variable: treatment number

Row variable	T1	T2	T3	T4	Total
Defect	11	16	12	4	43
No defect	40	34	31	41	146
Total	51	50	43	45	189

Expected frequencies
Column variable: treatment number

Row variable	T1	T2	T3	T4	Total
Defect	11.60	11.38	9.78	10.24	43
No defect	39.40	38.62	33.22	34.76	146
Total	51	50	43	45	189

Chi-square

Output level of significance	0.05
Number of rows	2
Number of columns	4
Degrees of freedom	3
Critical value	7.81
Chi-square test statistic	8.04
p-value	0.05

Reject the null hypothesis

Interpretation

The test value χ^2_{cal} > the critical value $\chi^2_{(0.05,3)}$, therefore we reject the null hypothesis and conclude that not all of the treatment types yield the same proportion of defects. Further analysis is required to identify which of the treatments are resulting in the highest proportion of defects. Improvement effort would therefore focus on the treatment(s) yielding the highest proportion of defects.

Gage R&R

Concepts

Gage R&R is a system used to validate the measurement system being used. Measurements should be precise and non-bias, repeatable, reproducible and stable. However, these criteria are frequently not met. Gage R&R is a set of trials conducted to assess the repeatability and reproducibility of the measurement system. In other words, in order to enable appropriate improvement strategies to be developed, Gage R&R is used to find out how much of the variation present is due to the measurement system and how much is real variation in the data.

Terminology

- A measurement system consists of measuring devices, procedures, definitions and operators.

- Bias is the difference between the observed average and the "standard" or reference value.

- Repeatability is the variation in multiple measurements obtained under repeatability conditions (same operator and same instrument measuring the identical characteristic on the same part within as small a time frame as possible) – not usually attainable.

- Reproducibility is the variation in the average of the measurements taken in the same way on the same item by multiple operators – not usually attainable.

- Gage R&R is the variation in multiple measurements made on the same part obtained under a wide range of conditions (different operators, different instruments, different days)

- Stability is the total variation in the measurements obtained on the same part over time. Stability is also referred to as drift.

Principles

1. The measurement must be made in *statistical control* or *statistical stability* (i.e. the variation from the measurement system is common cause only – not special cause).

2. The variation from the measurement system must be small compared with both the process and the specification limits.

3. Increments of measurement must be small relative to both process variability and specification limits.

4. Data must be sufficient. Each operator measures each unit repeatedly.

5. Data must be balanced. Each operator measures each unit the same number of times.

6. Data must be representative. The units tested should represent the full range of variation in the process.

7. Data must be accurate (unbiased). Operators should not know which unit they are measuring when they record their results – "blind testing".

Tests

1. Test for accuracy by repeatedly measuring known quantities.

2. Test for repeatability by having the same operator repeatedly measuring the same sample. This will reveal variation in the measurement device.

3. Test for reproducibility by having many operators repeatedly measuring the same sample.

4. Test for stability by having the same operator measure the same item over time.

Ensure that at least five distinct values are observed within the range of outcome variation for each of the tests.

Formulae

Analysis of variance (ANOVA) is used to measure the variance or standard deviation for each component of variability.

$$SD \text{ (repeatability)} = \text{residual SD}$$

The standard deviations due to operators, parts and operator–part interactions also need to be obtained using two-way ANOVA. The SD (reproducibility) represents the error over and above the SD (repeatability)

$$SD \text{ (reproducibility)} = \sqrt{SD_{operators}^2 + SD_{interaction}^2}$$

Gage R&R is the total error in the measurements:

$$SD \text{ (Gage R\&R)} = \sqrt{SD_{repeatability}^2 + SD_{reproducibility}^2}$$

$$\therefore \text{Gage R\&R} = 2 \times Z_\alpha \times SD \text{ (Gage R\&R)}$$

The variability in the process is calculated from the Gage R&R and the variation within the parts.

$$\text{total SD} = \sqrt{SD_{parts}^2 + SD_{Gage R\&R}^2}$$

Process capability and process sigma

Concepts

Process capability (see Figure A19) measures summarize how much variability there is in a process. These may be expressed as a relative measure. For example, process capability measures may be given relative to customer expectations or predetermined tolerances.

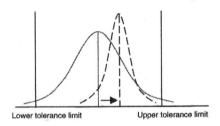

Lower tolerance limit   Upper tolerance limit

Figure A19

Process capability measures provide management with a statistical way of assessing and comparing the performance of processes. They are used to identify the impact of change over time and to focus improvement opportunities.

Increasing process capability decreases process variation. Examples include reducing the amount of rework and waste, and increasing predictability.

Process sigma can be applied to any process where the number of "defects" or "failures to meet specifications" can be counted. It can also be applied to multi-step processes where the aim is to measure overall process performance (see Figure A20).

Terminology

Process Sigma:	An expression of yield that is based on the number of defects per one million defect opportunities (DPMO).
Unit:	The item produced or the process outcome.
Defect:	Any unit that does not meet specification.
Defect opportunity:	A measurable chance for a defect to occur.

Methodology

1. Run the process being measured and record the number of defects.

2. Scale the number of defect opportunities (total number of process runs) up to 1 million.

3. Determine the yield for the process.

Sigma table (section)

Sigma	6	5.5	5	4.5	4	3.5	3	2.5	2	1.5	1	0.5
DPMO	3.4	32	8.5233	1,350	26,210	22,750	66,807	158,655	308,538	500,000	691,462	841,345
Yield (%)	99.99966	99.9968	99.977	99.87	99.38	97.7	93.3	84.1	69.1	50	30.9	15.9

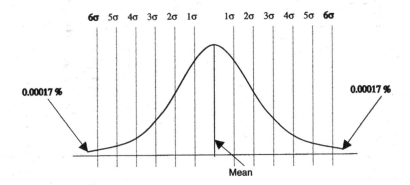

Figure A20 Normal distribution showing sigma values

Appendix 3

Glossary

Affinity chart/diagram This qualitative analysis technique is used to gather brainstorming data from the project team and to cluster common themes into logical groups. The affinity chart tool can be used to quickly gather and present the thoughts of a project team about a specific set of issues. The clustering can be further refined by prioritization techniques (such as merging, multi-voting and ranking) to create an agreed set of issues and priorities.

Alarm levels The upper or lower limits specified in a process that if exceeded will stimulate an alarm. Alarm levels should be set to ensure that they are sensitive to common problems but not over sensitive to acceptable levels of variation.

ANOVA – analysis of variance ANOVA is a statistical test of significance in the differences between samples for continuous data. The test is used to identify the significance of a factor in contributing to the overall variance. ANOVA can be used for comparing multiple groups. ANOVA allows project teams to understand how much of the variation in a process is caused by a significant factor and how much is caused by random noise.

Baseline The start point from which financial or other benefits are measured. It is very important to establish a clear and agreed baseline early in any project. The Finance department will usually play a key role in providing the data for a baseline and for signing off that the baseline is based on the correct financial data.

Benchmarking Benchmarking describes the processes and measures used to compare measured performance across companies and industries. Benchmarks are very useful in showing differing levels of performance. However, they must be handled carefully to ensure that what is being compared is similar – otherwise benchmarking can be a blunt instrument. Benchmarks are almost always quantitative measures. There are many benchmarking companies that can provide comparative statistics. However, project teams need to understand the background to the measures to ensure that they are relevant and robust.

Best in class   A term to describe the best measured practice across an organization or across all organizations in a sample. Best in class measures can be used as a goal or as a comparison of process capability. No organization can be best in class at everything so it is important to pick which processes need to be best in class and which can be sourced from a best in class service provider.

Best practices   A term to describe the best methods being used either within a company or by an external company. Generally, best practices will apply to processes. Some best practices will be capable of being measured and compared to make benchmarks. Some best practices are more difficult to measure but their use should be strongly encouraged and rewarded. Most companies would gain significant benefit just from applying best practices that are already in use in the company, more widely across the whole organization. Best practices are sometimes seen as lessons learned from one area of a business that could and should be applied more widely.

Black Belt   Black Belts are full time project managers of DMAIC and DFSS projects. They are trained in Six Sigma methods and tools. They have good statistical skills and a knowledge of when to applying them to specific business problems. Black Belts will typically have received four weeks of training and hands on Six Sigma application. Black Belts coach Green Belts and receive coaching from Master Black Belts. Black Belts are expected to have good facilitation skills in addition to their knowledge of process analysis and statistical tools.

BPR – business process re-engineering   BPR is a process consulting technique for analyzing and improving business processes within a business. It had its origins in the late 80s and early 1990s when consultants spotted the opportunity to improve cross functional process efficiency and effectiveness in large companies. The opportunities for BPR came from the existence of over rigid functional, organizational and geographic structures in large companies.

BPR set out to map "as-is" processes and then to develop "to be" processes for companies. BPR enjoyed some successes but successful implementation was patchy across companies and industries. Many companies found it difficult to really address cross functional issues. There are many similarities in the aims of Six Sigma and BPR projects.

Business case All projects however large or small should have a business case even if the likely financial benefits are negative. The business case has a number of purposes: (1) to highlight the likely costs and benefits of a proposed project; (2) to allow the project to be compared to other projects so that portfolio priorities can be established; (3) to justify the project; (4) to gain senior management support for funding and resources; (5) to enable ongoing support for the project; (6) to show the project team where they must look to secure the financial benefits from projects.

Capacity The number of units (at the right quality level) that a process can produce within a given time period. This is generally measured in absolute terms (e.g. 100,000 tonnes per month) or in percentage terms (e.g. working at 80% of capacity – actual production relative to potential capacity).

Cause and effect diagram This is a visual analytical tool (sometimes called a fishbone or Ishikawa diagram) that displays the grouped causes (fishbones) that contribute to a problem (the head of the fish). It is a very useful for illustrating the combination of factors that contribute to a problem. Most Six Sigma projects will require the project team to produce a root cause analysis. The iSS framework includes analytical tools to support fast and efficient development and display of Fishbone diagrams.

Champion see project sponsor.

Checklist or phase checklist Six Sigma project process management tools (e.g. DMAIC, DFSS) use a phase and gate approach. Each type of project is broken down into a number of phases and the project can only progress into the next phase if it passes the performance required by the phase checklist. Each question in the phase checklist is designed to stimulate the project manager and project sponsor to ask and answer the right level of questions. The questions are designed to be stretching and challenging in a positive way. The checklist for a phase should be reviewed by the team as it starts each phase because it defines what will need to be done to complete the phase. The aim of the checklists is to ensure that all key areas of a project, that can impact its success, are being addressed in parallel. No project should proceed to a new phase until the project manager has satisfied the project sponsor that the phase has been completed. This approach ensures that projects stay on track and planned financial benefits are delivered. The number and type of phases will vary depending on the nature of the project.

Chi-square test This is a quantitative analytical tool (chi rhymes with pie) that is used to compare discrete samples of data to determine whether they are significantly different e.g. performance of plant X versus plant Y, last week's performance against this week's. The chi-square test is used to test homogeneity and independence. It can be used to test "goodness of fit". The test generally sets out hypotheses and then tests whether the groups of data are homogeneous or independent.

Continuous data Continuous data is measured on a scale or continuum and is capable of being infinitely subdivided (e.g. 1.1, 1.11, 1.111) It is contrasted to discrete data which can only be into discrete elements (e.g. 1 car, 2 pumps). It is important to recognize the difference between continuous and discrete data when conducting statistical analysis.

Control charts A chart that is used to monitor/track changes in a process over time. It is intended to show whether a process is operating within upper and lower specification limits. The control chart enables people operating a process to see whether a variation in a data reading is acceptable or outside of acceptable limits.

Control phase The Control phase of projects is designed to ensure a smooth handover of solutions from the project team to process owners within the business. The control phase should occur in all Six Sigma projects (e.g. DMAIC and DFSS). It is critical that the project team ensures an effective handover and that the process owner is willing to accept the new process designs and alarm levels. During the Control phase the project team should also be recording lessons learned and gaining sign off of project completion from the project sponsor. At the end of the Control phase the project Sponsor and manager should ensure that all team members are recognized and rewarded for their efforts.

Conversion table This is a table that is used in Six Sigma to translate a number of defects per million opportunities (DPMO) into a sigma value. 3.4 DPMO converts to Six Sigma. 233 DPMO converts to five sigma. Six Sigma conversion tables are available in most Six Sigma books. They can also be calculated from normal distribution tables by adding 1.5 sigma to each Z-value. See also the Six Sigma calculator for details on how to calculate sigma values using spreadsheets.

CoPQ – cost of poor quality   This is a measure of the financial cost of poor quality in a process. Project teams study the impact of internal and external process problems and then quantify that impact. Typical contributors to the cost of poor quality are low value added activities (such as rework, quality inspections, expediting, unnecessary hand-offs) and customer dissatisfaction (such as lost orders, returns, late payments). CoPQ is a good measure to include in a project business case.

Correlation and correlation coefficient   Correlation is the level of linear relationship between two variables. Positive correlation means that they increase and decrease together. Negative correlation means that they move in opposite directions. The Correlation coefficient gives a specific value, usually between $+1$ and -1, to quantified the relationship.

CTQ – critical to quality   CTQ sets out the measurable elements of a process that are critical to achieving customer quality and satisfaction. The CTQ measures are designed to ensure that process improvement and innovation projects are fully aligned with those areas that are most valued by customers. Upper and lower specification limits are set on each CTQ measure to ensure that the project team is absolutely clear about the levels required by customers. CTQ measures should only be set with a high level of input from customers. Many organizations have been surprised to find from CTQ analysis that features and service levels that they have designed into products are simply not valued by customers. The key with CTQ is to listen to customers, measure what matters, set realistic limits and then to monitor achievement of CTQ targets.

Customer satisfaction   A key measure of how far products and services are meeting the requirements of customers. In assessing customer satisfaction it is critical to understand what actually matters to a customer.

Customer surveys   These are surveys of customers that are designed to gain qualitative and quantitative data on customer requirements. These can be a key input into all types of projects. They can help project teams with QFD and VOC analysis. Put simply, if you want to know what a customer values – ask them!

Cycle time   This is the total time it takes for a process from beginning to the end. Cycle time is made up of actual time spent on the process and delay time where the product or service is waiting to be worked on.

Data collection sheets   Data collection sheets are used in the Measure & Analyse phases of DMAIC and DFSS projects. They are designed to make data collection simple, standard and consistent. Project teams should take full advantage of existing data collection sheets and data sources. Data collection sheets and their content should be stored in the project data repository

Decision tree   A graphical representation of decision alternatives that can be used to show how decision options may vary under different sets of circumstances. It can be used for problem solving and to help people to decide on the best alternatives.

Defect   Any lack of conformance with intended quality standards where a product or service fails to meet customer requirements.

Defective   Any item that has one or more defects that do not meet intended quality standards

DFSS – Design for Six Sigma   DFSS is used for process innovation or creating new processes. It is used for two different types of situation; either creating a new process where no process currently exists or for making a radical process innovation which transforms current processes into totally new ways of doing activities. DFSS is typically used where DMAIC process improvement efforts cannot get beyond a five sigma level. DFSS is used to create the breakthrough and create the capability to operate processes at the Six Sigma level. There are different approaches to DFSS such as DMADV and DMADIC. DMADV stands for Define – Measure – Analyse – Design – Verify.

Discrete data   Discrete data is measured on a scale that is not infinitely divisible. It can only be divided into discrete elements (e.g. 1 car, 2 pumps). It is contrasted to Continuous data which is measured on a scale or continuum and is capable of being infinitely subdivided (e.g. 1.1, 1.11, 1.111) It is important to recognize the difference between continuous and discrete data when conducting statistical analysis.

DOE – design of experiments   DOE is a structured approach to understanding the impact of input factors (Xs) on the output (Y) of a process. Put simply, the aim is to vary the inputs in a systematic way to identify the key input factors that determine the output of a process. It is a way of evaluating the value of a factor or group of factors by controlling the process environment.

Downstream process   A process that is after the process being analysed (e.g. customer processes are often downstream from a company's processes but they may also initiate company processes)

DPMO – defects per million opportunities   DPMO is used in Six Sigma projects to calculate the level of sigma that a process or service is achieving. Six

Sigma is often defined as 3.4 DPMO. DPMO = (defects/number of opportunities) × 1,000,000

DPO – defects per opportunity DPO is the number of defects divided by the number of opportunities. DPO = defects/number of opportunities

Effectiveness Put simply, how well a process achieves what it is designed to do

Efficiency Put simply, how well a process maximizes output for a given set of inputs.

Error or experimental error A statistical term that measures the level of variation in data that cannot be attributed to the independent variables in an experiment. There can be multiple sources of error such as measurement bias or random effects.

Financial benefits These are the measurable and provable financial benefits that can be delivered from a successful project. They typically break down into operating cost savings, capital cost savings, revenue improvements, working capital changes and cost avoidance. Financial costs are usually easier to identify than revenue benefits. Financial benefits must be related to a financial baseline and linked into financial and budget numbers that are recognizable in profit and loss accounts and balance sheets.

Fishbone diagram see Cause and Effect diagram

Five Whys The Five Whys is a Japanese-originated technique for identifying the root cause of issues. The key is to pursue a connected thread of why questions to get to a real understanding about why a problem has occurred.

Flowchart see Process Map

FMEA – failure modes and effects analysis This is an advanced analytical tool that is used to identify potential failures in a process, product or service. It is a disciplined approach to identifying problems and then analyzing the likely frequency of problems, their impact and proposed response measures. The FMEA tool can be used by project teams to document their analysis and conclusions, and to allocate responsibilities for monitoring and addressing problem areas.

Forcefield analysis A visual analytical tool that is designed to show the positive and negative forces impacting a change within an organization. The positive or driving forces are represented as pushing against the negative or restraining forces. The iSS framework contains an automated tool for representing the conclusions of forcefield analysis simply and quickly.

Green Belts A Green Belt is a project team member who has received basic training in Six Sigma tools and techniques. This training will typically have been conducted over a 1–2 week period. Green Belts can be trusted to undertake most Six Sigma tasks and are the Black Belts of the future. Green Belts are coached and mentored by Black Belts and Master Black Belts.

Handover   The process of handing over responsibility for a process from one group to another. Most projects will inevitably involve the handing over of responsibility for solutions to a new process owner at the end of a project.

Histogram   A simple bar chart that is used to represent the frequency and distribution of data in groups. The chart can be used to visually represent data and to highlight the spread of data, the existence of outliers and the data that occurs most frequently. Stacked bar charts or histograms can also be used to show more information about the breakdown of data within the individual bars.

House of quality   see QFD.

Hypothesis and hypothesis testing   Hypothesis testing is used to focus attention on the suspected cause of a problem or opportunity and to test the validity of that suspicion. Within Hypothesis testing there are two types of Hypothesis: (1) the null hypothesis (H_0) – this generally states that there is no significant difference between sets of data; (2) the alternative hypothesis (H_a) – this states the alternative expectation of what differences between sets of data tells us about a sample. Statistical techniques are then applied to prove and/or disprove the null and alternative hypotheses. The aim is to use the data and statistical analysis techniques to show a statistically significant reason for accepting or rejecting hypotheses.

Input or input measure   The input to a process which can be described in terms of measures.

Ishikawa diagram   see cause and effect diagram.

ISO 9000   ISO 9000 is an international quality standard that sets standards of quality required in a company's processes. It relies on validating that processes are documented, exceptions acted upon and learning captured. There is an overlap with Six Sigma in the desire for high levels of quality. The challenge facing ISO 9000 is that it can end up being a documentation exercise that rewards conformance rather than results. Six Sigma requires a greater focus on results, e.g. defects of less than 3.4 parts per million (p.p.m.) as a target. The iSS framework is designed to allow Six Sigma improvements whilst also creating a "light touch" mechanism for documenting and proving ISO 9000 process standards. As such it is a good mechanism for addressing both requirements without unnecessary additional effort.

KPIs – key performance indicators   KPIs are designed to focus attention on achieving performance targets that will deliver critical success factors. KPIs should focus on actions, they should be measurable, they must be timely, owned in the organization and controllable. They should be set at multiple levels within a firm. Integrating and linking different levels of KPIs can be an effective way of encouraging employees to work co-operatively together. This approach must be used carefully because artificial linkages and KPI systems can cause unexpected problems and behavior.

Lessons learned   Lessons learned should be recorded and shared from all projects. No project should be signed off by its sponsor as complete until lessons learned have been recorded. All lessons learned are then screened by the portfolio team an assessed to see whether they should become best practices. Lessons learned are all retained in the overall projects data repository.

Low hanging fruit   A term to describe financial or other benefits that are easy to deliver quickly. The analogy uses the idea of fruit that is easy for people to pick and eat. Many organizations will claim that most of the "low hanging fruit" was taken a long time ago. Some organizations have "low hanging fruit" that cannot be taken because of internal political issues or because commonly used approaches to projects make it difficult to deliver these types of benefits.

Master Black Belt   Master Black Belts are more experienced Black Belts. They take responsibility for helping multiple Six Sigma projects to be successful. They are skilled in both the DMAIC and DFSS processes. They act as coaches to Black Belts and Green Belts in helping them to be successful on projects. Master Black Belts are expected to play a key role in developing new techniques for improving and transforming company processes. They are capable of teaching Six Sigma methodologies and applying the most complex integrated Six Sigma analysis tools.

Measurement systems analysis – MSA   MSA is a quantitative method for determining how much of the variation within a process is due to the variation within a measurement process.

MINITAB   MINITAB is a leading statistical analysis package. It has the capability to conduct most different types of statistical analysis required on Six Sigma projects. It usually requires training in the use of the tools even for people with a good background in statistics. It has more powerful tools than the statistical capabilities generally found in spreadsheet packages. A range of statistical tools used on a Six Sigma projects can be saved within a single MINTAB workbook.

MTBF – mean time between failures. This is the average time between failure for a process. It is a measure of the level of quality of a process.

Non-value-added activities These are the opposite of value added activities. They can be defined as activities that do not create value for either the company or its customers. The "value-added" test can be stated simply at five levels: (1) Do customers value this process/activity? (2) Are they willing to pay for us to do this? (3) Can we do this process profitably? (4) Can we do this process right, first time? (5) Does the process cause a meaningful change in the customer experience?

Normal distribution This is a statistical distribution where the mean and median are the same and data is distributed evenly around the mean. The normal distribution is a regular bell-shaped curve. The standard deviation or sigma can be looked up using a normal distribution table. Six Sigma tables are an adaptation of the normal distribution with a shift of 1.5 sigma (e.g. 4.5 sigma in the normal distribution is equal to Six Sigma (e.g. 3.4 defects per million)

Objective/goal statement A clear and unambiguous statement of what a project or project phase will achieve. The best objective/goal statements are simple and focused. They should include performance targets that success can be measured against.

Operational data definition A clear and concise definition of a term. It is important that project teams should state their data definitions (and use existing data definitions as far as possible). This ensures that everyone is working off common definitions and looking at the same data.

Opportunity costs Opportunity cost can be described as the cost of not doing the next best activity. For instance, the opportunity cost of a project is the benefits that cannot be achieved by doing the next highest priority project. (The opportunity cost of allocating a person to a project is the benefits that cannot be achieved by them doing the next best activity.)

Output measure The output from a process which can be described in terms of measures

Pareto chart The Pareto chart combines a bar chart with a cumulative distribution. This allows project teams to see whether the Pareto principle is present in the data (e.g. 80% of issues are described by 20% of the causes).

Pareto principle Simply stated, 80% of a task can be achieved by focusing on

20% of the required activities. The Pareto principle focuses attention on the vital key factors. Project teams can make faster progress by applying the Pareto principle. The opposite of Pareto is sometimes described as "trying to boil the ocean". Project managers and teams need to satisfy themselves that they are applying the Pareto principle effectively (e.g. not too much but not too little effort).

PDCA – plan, do, check, act A simple approach to managing changes in an organization. The aim is that all changes should be planned, then implemented, checked for effectiveness and efficiency and any required changes acted upon. The approach was advocated by Deming as a key way to ensure data driven process improvements.

Performance measures see KPIs.

Phase checklist see Checklist.

Poka yoke Mistake proofing a process by focusing on potential problems before they occur. This is a Japanese term and method designed to design out potential problems. This is particularly important when it is critical that processes do not fail, e.g. a nuclear power plant.

Precision The level of accuracy that is applied to a measure. The level of precision should be appropriate to the process being measured, e.g. "customer service is good" is not precise but "95.4% of customers were very satisfied with delivery performance" is more precise.

Probability A numerical assessment of the likelihood that an event will occur.

Problem/opportunity statement A clear and unambiguous statement of the problem/opportunity that will be addressed by a project. Put simply, what is the problem that the project is trying to address? It is important to check that the proposed project and solution will address the underlying problem/opportunity that was the reason for the project. It is surprising to find that this is not the case on many projects.

Process A series of activities that when combined lead to the delivery of a product or service that will satisfy customer needs

Process capability This is a capability of a process to deliver a product or service without defects. In simple terms how well a process will perform an ongoing basis given the current design of the process.

Process design The overall design of the steps and activities within a process.

Process innovation The creation of new (often radically new) processes to address a customer requirement. Within integrated Six Sigma (iSS) process innovation projects are addressed using a Design for Six Sigma (DFSS)

approach. Process innovation is often required where process improvements cannot move a process beyond five sigma levels of quality.

Process management Any activity that involves the modification, redesign and improvement of a process to deliver increased value. Process management involves the proactive management of processes and should require continuous innovation.

Process map/flowchart A visual analytical tool that is designed to enable project teams to map and analyse processes at differing levels of detail. The process maps allows key steps to be mapped out to increase the project teams understanding of key flows and six key factors; inventory, costs, revenues, working capital, time and quality measures. Process mapping should also focus on areas such as the number of steps, number of physical handovers and the value of activities. Physical process flow charting is often referred to as a brown paper/post-it note exercise (from the roll of paper used to stick post-it notes to). Automated flowcharting can be created using packages such as Excel, PowerPoint and Visio. Project teams should be careful to focus attention on the right level of detail and critical process measures. SIPOC diagrams are a type of process maps.

Process measures Clear measures that unambiguously define the requirements for successful execution of a process

Process owner The individual who has responsibility for a specific process. Project teams that are improving or designing new processes must hand over the new process design to a process owner before the project is completed. Process owners should be involved in projects at an early stage to avoid later rework.

Process redesign The redesign of a business process. This can involve an improvement to the process or in some cases it may involve the design of a radical new process.

Process re-engineering see BPR – business process re-engineering.

Project charter A clearly stated summary of the objectives and key elements of a project. All Six Sigma projects must have an agreed project charter that is developed in the define phase.

Project data repository The project data repository works at two levels: (1) a single location where all data from a single project is held and made available to the project team; (2) A single overall repository of data from all projects linked to a portfolio knowledge base. Over time, the project data repository should grow into a valuable asset for any company.

Project manager The individual who has responsibility for the successful delivery of financial and other benefits from a project. There should only be one overall project manager for a specific project. Great project managers are good at a range of skills and activities but above all they are good at managing project risks, setting realistic objectives and timescales, managing their resources carefully and getting the best out of their teams. Project management requires a combination of knowledge, skills and experience. Great project managers lead by example and are recognized for their ability to develop their people. The best project managers have a quiet confidence that builds trust and commitment into project successes. Good project managers are like an umbrella in protecting their teams.

Project plan The plan of activities, tasks, timescales and responsibilities for a project. All projects must have a robust plan that is effectively executed. Good project managers and teams should "Plan the work, then work the plan". Project plans should be documented using software such as Excel, or MS Project. Sophisticated project management software, such as Artemis, is available for very complex projects. For most Six Sigma projects Excel is usually sufficient. MS Project is a more robust software tool than Excel that can be used for projects that are too complex for Excel but do not require Artemis-type capabilities.

Project sponsor The sponsor or champion of a project. This role is designed to provided "top cover" for a project. Great project sponsors know how to ask the right questions and when they are needed to ensure the success of projects. The role of the project sponsor is to champion a project, to promote the project to the wider business and to ensure that it remains on track. The role of the sponsor is not to do the project, however interesting. Great project sponsors know how to spend the right amount of time with the project manager and team. They are usually very good at picking out the difficult questions that no-one has covered off but which represents a significant problem or opportunity for the project. Great project sponsors are not inactive or absent. They somehow know when they are required and the difference between sponsorship and interference. Good project sponsors are like an umbrella protecting their project managers and teams.

Quality A term that is used to describe the level of excellence of a process. In the past, quality was often defined in terms of conformance to specified standards. This definition is often seen to be too narrow. More recent definitions of quality focus on the ability of a process to consistently deliver satisfaction to the customer and value to the provider.

Quality function deployment QFD (sometimes known as the "house of quality") is a structured methodology that is used to identify and prioritize customer needs and then translate them into process activities. QFD is a Japanese quality approach that has been adapted to Six Sigma. QFD's use is particularly important in Design for Six Sigma (DFSS) projects.

Random sampling The process of sampling where data points are selected totally at random. This approach to sampling is designed to reduce sampling bias. It is important to check for sampling bias when setting up collection methods for random sampling.

Regression A statistical analysis technique that is used to determine the relationship between a set of independent variables (Xs) and the dependent variable (Y). Regression analysis goes beyond scatter diagrams to establish a more precise understanding about the relationships between variables. The availability of regression analysis software tools and significance tests (such as R^2 and correlation coefficients) means that regression analysis is becoming a more mainstream analysis tool in Six Sigma projects.

Repeatability The ability of a single person to obtain the same result each time data is collected and analysed. Repeatability is a measure of consistency and stability of a data measurement and analysis process.

Reproducibility The ability of multiple people to obtain the same results each time data is collected and analysed. Reproducibility is a measure of consistency and stability of a data measurement and analysis process.

Rework loops These are points in a process where problems are identified and passed backwards (or upstream) in a process to allow rework to be conducted. Rework should be minimized in an overall process and it is a key area for project teams to investigate in a DMAIC project.

Risk analysis The process of analyzing risks by a project team. The Six Sigma process should contain an automated set of tools for identifying, prioritizing and summarizing risks. It also requires project teams to show how these risks are being addressed and how they are changing over time. A key role of the project sponsor is to ensure that key risks are identified and addressed. Some project risks are likely to be beyond the control of a project team. The team should work with the project sponsor to address these risks where it is possible. Risks are often broken down into controllable risks (e.g. risks that the project team can manage) and uncontrollable risks that are more difficult to address but must be recognized.

Run chart see Control chart.

Sampling Sampling is the process of using a smaller subset of data within an overall population to represent a larger population. It is important because it enables project teams to draw conclusions about data without having to analyse all the data. Acceptable sample sizes can be calculated using statistical techniques.

Sampling bias Sampling Bias is the impact of factors that causes a sample to be more or less valid. Bias is present in all samples, the objective is to sample in a way that keeps bias to a minimum. A sample that is not valid due to bias is described as a Biased sample. It is important for project teams to design a sampling approach that minimizes bias.

Scatter plot/diagram A graph or diagram to show the relationship between two variables. This relationship is usually described as the correlation between the two variables. The scatter diagram can show a relationship between variables but it cannot be used to show causality. The scatter diagram allows conclusion to be drawn about the type of relationship between variables [e.g. positive (they move up together) or negative (they move in opposite directions)]. Also look at correlation and correlation coefficients.

Scope Scope defines the areas that will be looked at within a project (i.e. in scope) as well as the areas that will be excluded (i.e. out of scope). Scope can be defined by terms such as process, function, geography (e.g. outside USA) or organizational entity (e.g. plant, sales organization). Scope definition is a critical thing to get right. Too broad a scope often leads to lack of focus and project teams attempting to "boil the ocean". Too narrow a scope can seriously limit a team's ability to draw meaningful and complete solutions. The project manager and project sponsor are responsible for the correct definition of scope.

SIPOC diagram SIPOC stands for Supplier – Input – Process – Output – Customer. SIPOC is a qualitative analytical tool that is designed to focus a project team's attention on the key activities involved in a process that flows between a company, its suppliers and customers. It is a combination of process mapping with recording of key inputs and outputs of processes. The output from a SIPOC diagram should be a list of key insights about problems and opportunities.

SPC – statistical process control This is the application of statistical control techniques (such as control charts and alarm levels) to manage variation within a process. SPC has been in existence for many years and is widely used as a mechanism for identifying and addressing performance problems mainly in manufacturing.

Specification limits The upper and lower performance limits that are specified for a particular process. The objective of the specification limits is to highlight non-conformance and to identify trends in data that may lead to a process moving outside acceptable performance levels.

Stratification The process of breaking data down into groups based on specific criteria. Criteria could includes areas such as type of data (e.g. invoices, production reports, customer service complaints), time (e.g. day, week, month, quarter), location (e.g. plant, country, region) and owner (e.g. function, department, entity). Stratification is important in Six Sigma because it enables teams to create much greater visibility around what is going on in a process.

Stratified sampling In stratified sampling the data is first segmented into sub-groups or strata. Then a sample is taken from each sub-group for analysis and comparison. This technique is particularly useful for data sets where there is a large population with multiple groupings.

SWOT analysis This is a qualitative analysis tool designed to assess a company's competitive environment. SWOT stands for Strengths – Weaknesses – Opportunities and Threats. The aim is for the project team to construct a 2 × 2 matrix including each of the four areas. It is recommended that each segment of the matrix should not exceed 10 bullet points.

Systematic sampling Systematic sampling is a method used to obtain a regular sample from a population. It is used in Six Sigma activities to obtain structured data based on time within a process. Systematic samples can be taken at a time interval (e.g. every 1 hour) or as part of a process flow (e.g. every 100 items or every 500 invoices).

t-test The *t*-test is used to determine statistical significance between two sets of continuous data. It tests the statistical significance of differences between the groups. It is often used with sample sizes less than 30 when the normal distribution is not effective.

Taguchi method This method is similar to design of experiments (DOE). It is a technique for focusing attention on how particular combinations of variables can be used to identify the individual impact of variables. The Taguchi method is often applied to designing and executing experiments in customer satisfaction over a period of service time.

To be process mapping The mapping of new or future processes. "To be" refers to what the processes are meant to look like in the future.

TQM – total quality management TQM is a management philosophy and set of practices designed to continuously improve the performance of organizational processes, products and services, in order to satisfy customers and profitability. TQM focuses attention on the quality of processes from its suppliers' supplier through a company to its customers' customers. The objective is to achieve zero defects and to minimize unnecessary process variation. The theory of TQM is powerful but its implementation has sometimes been criticized for being too mechanistic and focused on documentation rather than results. Six Sigma builds on TQM but is more focused on results and creating a culture of continuous innovation.

Transactional Six Sigma Transactional refers to use of Six Sigma outside its traditional manufacturing environment, e.g. in back office functions or financial institutions. The focus in transactional Six Sigma shifts to applying techniques, that have been developed in manufacturing, to the hidden transaction factories that are present in many large organizations. It covers areas such as invoicing, call centres and financial services.

Upstream process A process that is before the process being analysed (e.g. supplier processes are generally upstream from a company's processes)

Value-added activities These can be defined as activities that create value for both the company and its customers. They can be contrasted with non-value added activities that do not create such value. The "value added" test can be stated simply at five levels: (1) Do customers value this process/activity? (2) Are they willing to pay for us to do this? (3) Can we do this process profitably? (4) Can we do this process right, first time? (5) Does the process cause a meaningful change in the customer experience?

Variance In statistical terms, the variance is the square of the standard deviation. It measures the spread of data around the mean.

Variation This is the level of fluctuation or change in a process. It is measured by looking at the average spread of data around the mean. It gives a good indication of the level of stability or predictability of a process. Low variation is generally good, high variation is not. Variation can be caused by a variety of internal and external factors that may or may not be controllable. The variation should also be looked at to understand the distribution of data around the Mean. Six Sigma generally assumes a normal or uniform distribution of data around the Mean. Process improvements or innovations should aim to reduce the level of variation.

VOC – voice of the customer   VOC is a qualitative analysis tool that is used to translate what customers say into clear customer requirements and measurement mechanisms. The tool recognizes that customers comments may often not be a good reflection of what they actually need. The tool helps a project team to work out customer needs and to agree requirements and measures. VOC data can be obtained from interviews, surveys, warranty claims, returns, customer service complaints, sales people and focus groups.

X X is often described as the independent or input variables. The relationship between the X variables and Y (the output variable) is a key task of Six Sigma project teams. Most of the quantitative analytical tools used in Six Sigma are focused on increasing understanding of statistically significant relationships between X and Y variables. Such analysis supports fact-based problem solving.

Y Y is often described as the dependent variable that is impacted by the X variable(s). It is generally used to show the output of a process/activity and its dependence on input factors. It is commonly represented in equations as a function of the X variables, e.g. $Y = f(X)$. A Y-axis is one of two axes used to map relationships between variables in a graph or chart.

Yield metrics/first pass and final   Yield is the proportion of a process/ units that have zero defects. It is measured in percentage terms (e.g. 98.7%). In transactional Six Sigma, Yield can sometimes be defined as the percentage of commitments met successfully out of the total number of opportunities. Yield is sometimes broken down into sub areas such as first-pass yield and final yield. First pass yield is the percentage number of items that passed through the process first time without defects. Final yield is the percentage number of items that passed through the process after rework. These measures can be important in understanding and identifying more complex causes of process variability. Yield can sometimes be measured as defects per million opportunities (DPMO) (this is base input into a Six Sigma performance calculator).

Bibliography

Bisgard, S., "Industrial use of statistically designed experiments: case study references and some historical anecdotes," *Quality Enigineering*, vol. 4 (1992).

Brassard, Michael and Diane Ritter, *Sailing Through Six Sigma*.

Breyfogle, F. W., *Managing Six Sigma*.

Breyfogle, F. W., *Implementing Six Sigma: Smarter Solutions Using Statistical Methods*, 2nd edn.

Chowdhury, Subir, *The Power of Six Sigma: An Inspiring Tale of How Six Sigma Is Transforming the Way We Work*.

Ehrlich, Betsi Harris, *Transactional Six Sigma and Lean Servicing: Leveraging Manufacturing Concepts to Achieve World-class Service*.

Eureka, W. E. and N. E. Ryan, *The Customer-driven Company*. ASI Press (1988).

George, Michael L., *Lean Six Sigma: Combining Six Sigma Quality with Lean Production Speed*.

Goh, T. N., "An efficient empirical approach to process improvement," *International Journal of Quality and Reliability Management*, vol. 6, no. 1 (1993).

Goh, T. N., "Perspectives on statistical quality engineering," *TQM Magazine*, vol. 11 (1999).

Hahn, G. J. "The impact of Six Sigma improvement – a glimpse into the future of statistics," *American Statistics*, vol. 53 (1999).

Harry, Mikel J., *et al.*, *Six Sigma: The Breakthrough Management Strategy Revolutionizing the World's Top Corporations.*

Henderson, K. and J. Evans, "Successful implementation of Six Sigma: benchmarking: General Electric Company," *Benchmarking and International Journal*, vol. 7 (2000).

Hendricks, C. and R. Kelbaugh, "Implementing Six Sigma at GE," *Journal of Quality and Participation*, vol 21. (1998).

Ishikawa, K., *Guide to Quality Control.* Asian Productivity Organization, Tokyo (1976).

Keller, Paul A., *Six Sigma Deployment: A Guide for Implementing Six Sigma in Your Organization.*

Pande, Peter S., *The Six Sigma Way: How GE, Motorola, and Other Top Companies are Honing Their Performance.*

Pande, Peter S. *et al.*, *What Is Six Sigma?*

Pyzdek, Thomas, *The Six Sigma Handbook, Revised and Expanded: The Complete Guide for Greenbelts, Blackbelts, and Managers at All Levels.*

TQM Magazine, "Critical success factors for the implementation of Six Sigma projects in organizations," vol. 14 (2002).

Index

hypothesis/hypothesis testing 258
  concepts 235–6
  t-test 236–8

Improve phase 105–6
  checklist 124–8
  communications plans 119–24
  pilot phase 110–14
  solution definition/business case
      114–19
  solution options/filter 107–10
  solution risk summary 119
Individual Contribution and Rewards
      Statement (ICRS) 140–1
input/input measure 258
Isaac, Max 56
Ishikawa diagram *see* cause and effect
      diagram
Ishikawa, K. 51
ISO 9000 258–9
issue trees
  concepts 201
  good practices 203
  methodology 202–3

Jackson, Jesse 149
Jay, Anthony 35
Jonson, Samuel 29
Juran, Joseph 132

Kelbaugh, R. 63
key performance indicators (KPIs) 16,
      17–19, 259
knowledge 159–61
KPIs *see* key performance indicators

Lao Tzu 69

leadership 147, 149–50
lessons learned 259
  control phase 134, 136–9
  define phase 48–50
low hanging fruit 259

McBurnie, Anton 56
McNerney, Jim 131
McNerney, W. James 154
Master Black Belt (MBB) 68, 71,
      86–7, 96, 100–2, 107, 109,
      124, 125, 141, 142, 163, 184,
      187, 259
mean time between failures (MTBF)
      260
Measure & Analyse 69–71
  advanced tools 95–6
  baseline performance 81–3
  basic qualitative tools 88–92
  basic quantitative tools 92–5
  best practices/benchmarks 83–4
  checklist 100–4
  data analysis 84–7
  data collection activities 71–9
  DFSS 181–2
  drawing out conclusions 98–100
  sigma levels/process capability 80–1
  tool selection matrix 96–8
measurement systems analysis (MSA)
      259
Mees, Allan 137
MINITAB 87, 259–60
moments-of-truth (MoT) analysis
  concepts 203–4
  good practices 205
  methodology 204–5
Moore, Dudley 182

Sigma Conversion Table (with 1.5 Shift)

Yield (%)	DPMO	Sigma
6.68	933200	0.00
10.56	894400	0.25
15.87	841300	0.50
22.66	773400	0.75
30.85	691500	1.00
40.13	598700	1.25
50.00	500000	1.50
59.87	401300	1.75
69.15	308500	2.00
77.34	226600	2.25
84.13	158700	2.50
89.44	105600	2.75
93.32	66800	3.00
95.99	40100	3.25
97.73	22700	3.50
98.78	12200	3.75
99.38	6200	4.00
99.70	3000	4.25
99.87	1350	4.50
99.94300	570	4.75
99.97700	230	5.00
99.99120	88	5.25
99.99680	32	5.50
99.99895	10.5	5.75
99.99966	3.4	6.00

Printed and bound by CPI Group (UK) Ltd, Croydon, CR0 4YY

13/04/2025

14656466-0001